Grammar
Step by Step
Teacher's Manual

1

Helen Kalkstein Fragiadakis
Ellen Rosenfield

with Chants by Carolyn Graham

Grammar Step by Step 1 Teacher's Manual

Published by McGraw-Hill ESL/ELT, a business unit of The McGraw-Hill Companies, Inc., 1221 Avenue of the Americas, New York, NY 10020. Copyright ©2004 by the McGraw-Hill Companies, Inc. All rights reserved. Permission is granted to reproduce these materials as needed for classroom use or for use by individual students. Distribution for sale is prohibited.

Some ancillaries, including electronic and print components, may not be available to customers outside the United States.

1 2 3 4 5 6 7 8 9 10 QPD 10 09 08 07 06 05 04

ISBN: 0-07-284521-X

Editorial director: Tina B. Carver
Executive editor: Erik Gundersen
Senior developmental editor: Mari Vargo
Developmental editor: Jennifer Monaghan
Director of North American marketing: Thomas P. Dare
Director of international marketing and sales: Kate Oakes
Editorial assistant: David Averbach
Production manager: Juanita Thompson
Cover designer: Delgado and Company, Inc.
Interior designer: Wee Design Group
Art: Artists from IllustrationOnLine.com

www.esl-elt.mcgraw-hill.com

The McGraw-Hill Companies

Table of Contents

Expansion Activity

Review Tests

Answer Keys

To the Teacher

Grammar Step by Step 1 is the first in a three-level series of beginning to high intermediate books offering extensive grammar practice for young adult and adult learners. The *Grammar Step by Step* Teacher's Manual, a valuable resource for teachers, contains reproducible Expansion Activities and Review Tests and an Answer Key for each component.

The Teacher's Manual greatly reduces teacher prep time by offering a review test for each group of Student Book lessons, for a total of fifteen two-page tests. The 64 reproducible Expansion Activities, one for each two-page lesson in the Student Book, offer additional practice on the grammar points covered in the Student Book. Teachers and students working in an intensive instructional setting can take advantage of the wealth of Expansion Activities in the Teacher's Manual to supplement the Student Book materials. Alternately, teachers can assign the expansion activities for homework or extra practice to meet the individual needs of students. The Answer Keys at the back of the Teacher's Manual cover Student Book lessons, Expansion Activities, and Review Tests.

Expansion Activity
Nouns

Name _____ Date _____

A Write five singular nouns from Lesson 1.

_____ apartment _____

_____

_____

_____

_____

B Show your nouns to a partner. Working with your partner, write *a* or *an* before each of the nouns you wrote above.

_____ an apartment _____

_____

_____

_____

_____

C Now, work with your partner again and make the nouns plural.

_____ apartments _____

_____

_____

_____

_____

Expansion Activity
Proper Nouns and Subject Pronouns

Name _____ Date _____

A Look at the words. Capitalize the proper nouns.

M
~~m~~ike   a table   paris   bedrooms   helen

sony™   a sofa   mexico   disneyland™   books

star wars™   doors   elizabeth   pepsi™   a kitchen

B Write each proper noun in the correct box.

People	Places	Things
Mike		

C Find a partner. Compare your answers. Then add two nouns to each box above.

LESSON

3

Expansion Activity
Adjectives

Name _____ Date _____

A Fill in the blanks with as many adjectives as you can.

EXAMPLE: _happy_   **man**   ___4___ adjectives

old   _tall_

sad   _____

1. _____   **car**   _____ adjectives

    _____   _____

    _____   _____

2. _____   **house**   _____ adjectives

    _____   _____

    _____   _____

3. _____   **student**   _____ adjectives

    _____   _____

    _____   _____

4. _____   **movie**   _____ adjectives

    _____   _____

    _____   _____

B Fill in the blanks with the number of adjectives above. Then add the numbers together.

1. _____ + 2. _____ + 3. _____ + 4. _____ = _____ Total

Expansion Activity
Verbs

Name _____ Date _____

A Read the paragraph. Circle the verbs.

My name (is) Anna. I live in Chicago. I go to school. At school, I study English. I read books. On Saturday and Sunday, I sleep. Then, I run and swim. I go to parties. I love Chicago!

B Fill in each space below with one of the choices below.

In the house   For fun   At school   On Saturdays   On Mondays

1. _____ , I study.

2. _____ , I swim.

3. _____ , I cook.

4. _____ , I dance.

5. _____ , I go to a party.

6. _____ , I sleep.

7. _____ , I write.

8. _____ , I talk.

Expansion Activity

BE—Affirmative Statements (Subject Pronouns)

Name _____ Date _____

A Read the sentences. Circle the forms of the verb *BE* (*am, is, are*).

1. I (am) a teacher.

2. They're happy together.

3. My sister is a soccer player.

4. We are at school every day.

5. I'm 16 years old.

6. You are from Chicago.

7. He's an architect.

8. It is big.

9. You're tall.

10. We are twins

B Look at the sentences in Exercise A. Write the sentences again. Change the pronouns and forms of the verb *BE*.

1. (She) _____She is a teacher_____

2. (We) _____

3. (I) _____

4. (He) _____

5. (You) _____

6. (They) _____

7. (I) _____

8. (They) _____

9. (She) _____

10. (You) _____

Expansion Activity
BE—Negative Statements

Name _____ Date _____

A Read the paragraph about Anna's School. Underline the forms of *BE*.

Anna's School

My school <u>is</u> beautiful. It's in a new building. The classes are interesting. The teachers are good. My teacher is early every day. My room is nice. The students are friendly. I am busy every day. I'm happy at my school.

B Now make the sentences in the paragraph negative to describe Mike's school.

Mike's School

My school isn't beautiful.

_____

_____

_____

_____

_____

_____

_____

LESSON 7

Expansion Activity

BE with Adjectives and Nouns (Plurals)

Name _____ Date _____

A Write five sentences about the picture. Use the verb *BE* with adjectives and nouns.

EXAMPLE: The people are noisy

1. _____

_____

2. _____

_____

3. _____

_____

4. _____

_____

5. _____

_____

B Show your sentences to a partner. Work together to correct the grammar.

Expansion Activity
BE with Frequency Adverbs

Name _____ Date _____

A Fill in the blanks to make *true* sentences about you. Use *always, usually, often, sometimes,* or *never.*

EXAMPLE: I am _____*never*_____ late for class.

1. I am _____ late for class.

2. I am _____ home on Saturdays.

3. On Mondays, I am _____ busy.

4. On Saturdays and Sundays, I _____ go to restaurants.

5. I am _____ tired.

6. My home is _____ quiet.

7. I am _____ friendly.

8. In class, I am _____ noisy.

9. On weekends, I _____ go to the movies.

10. I am _____ absent from school.

B Read your sentences from Exercise A to a partner. Write five sentences about your partner.

EXAMPLE: *Elena is sometimes late for class.*

1. _____

2. _____

3. _____

4. _____

5. _____

LESSON 9

Expansion Activity
There is/There are

Name _____ Date _____

A Read the sentences. Fill in the blanks to make *true* sentences about you. Then circle the correct words in parentheses.

EXAMPLE: There (is/are) _____2_____ (pillow /pillows) on my bed.

1. There (is/are) _____ (student/students) in my class.

2. There (is/are) _____ (teacher/teachers) in my class.

3. There (is/are) _____ (person/people) in my family.

4. There (is/are) _____ (chair/chairs) in my kitchen.

5. There (is/are) _____ (television/televisions) in my home.

6. There (is/are) _____ (room/rooms) in my home.

7. There (is/are) _____ (desk/desks) in my class.

8. There (is/isn't) a night table next to my bed.

9. There (is/isn't) a dresser in the corner of my bedroom.

10. There (is/isn't) a television in my class.

11. There (are/aren't) flowers in front of my school.

B Now write five more sentences about yourself.

1. _____
   _____

2. _____
   _____

3. _____
   _____

4. _____
   _____

5. _____
   _____

Expansion Activity

BE—Yes-No Questions and Short Answers

Name _____ Date _____

A Read the questions. Circle the answer that is true for you.

EXAMPLE: Are you a student?

(Yes, I am.)   No, I'm not.

1. Are you a man?

   Yes, I am.   No, I'm not.

2. Are you a woman?

   Yes, I am.   No, I'm not.

3. Is your teacher a woman?

   Yes, she is.   No, he isn't.

4. Is your teacher a man?

   Yes, he is.   No, she isn't.

5. Are you married?

   Yes, I am.   No, I'm not.

6. Are you an actor?

   Yes, I am.   No, I'm not.

7. Are you a student?

   Yes, I am.   No, I'm not.

8. Is your classroom big?

   Yes, it is.   No, it isn't.

9. Are you from Asia?

   Yes, I am.   No, I'm not.

10. Are you from South America?

    Yes, I am.   No, I'm not.

B Find a partner. Ask your partner the questions from Exercise A.

LESSON 11

Expansion Activity
Is there and *Are there*

Name _____ Date _____

A Answer the questions below. Write complete sentences.

EXAMPLE: Are there a lot of books in your class?

_____Yes, there are._____

1. Are there desks in your class?

_____

2. Is there a television in your class?

_____

3. Are there women in your class?

_____

4. Is there a computer in your class?

_____

5. Is there a computer in your home?

_____

6. Are there a lot of kids in your neighborhood?

_____

7. Are there usually a lot of cars in your neighborhood?

_____

8. Are there sometimes noisy children in your neighborhood?

_____

B Write one new question. Then write the answer.

Question: _____

_____

Answer: _____

_____

Expansion Activity
Demonstrative Pronouns
This and *That*

Name _____ Date _____

A Read the sentences. Fill in the blanks with *This is* or *That's*.

1. There is a great street entertainer down the street.

_____*That's*_____ a great street entertainer.

2. You are in a really good restaurant.

_____ a really good restaurant.

3. You are near a big supermarket.

_____ a big supermarket.

4. There's a nice school across the street.

_____ a nice school.

5. You are next to a large tree.

_____ a large tree.

6. There is a large statue two blocks away.

_____ a large statue.

7. You are in front of the library.

_____ the library.

8. You are in a beautiful park.

_____ a beautiful park.

9. You are far from City Hall.

_____ City Hall.

10. There's a bank across the street.

_____ a bank.

Expansion Activity
Demonstrative Pronouns
These and *Those*

Name _____ Date _____

A Circle *These are* or *Those are*.

EXAMPLE: There are big statues across the street.

(These are/(Those are)) big statues.

1. You are on your bed. Your shoes are in the closet.

(These are/Those are) my shoes.

2. Two books are in your hands.

(These are/Those are) my books.

3. You are near two pillows.

(These are/Those are) my pillows.

4. There are two street entertainers across the street.

(These are/Those are) great entertainers!

5. You are between two big trees.

(These are/Those are) big trees.

6. Your sisters are one block away.

(These are/Those are) my sisters.

7. You are near some beautiful flowers.

(These are/Those are) beautiful flowers.

8. You are across the street from a park with two ugly statues.

(These are/Those are) ugly statues.

9. You are close to your grandparents.

(These are/Those are) my grandparents.

10. Your parents are across the street.

(These are/Those are) my parents.

LESSON **14**

Expansion Activity
Demonstrative Pronouns
This, That, These, and *Those*

Name _____ Date _____

A Read the paragraph. Circle *this, that, these* and *those.*

Look at (this) picture. It's my bedroom. Over there is my closet. That's my <u>shirt</u>. That's my <u>shoe</u>. That's my <u>toy</u>. Look here on my bed. This is my <u>book</u>. This is my <u>pillow</u>. Look near the door. That's my <u>sister</u>.

B Rewrite the paragraph. Change the underlined nouns from singular to plural. Change *this is* and *that is* to *these are* and *those are.*

Look at this picture. It's my bedroom. Over there is my closet. Those are my shirts. _____

_____

_____

_____

_____

_____

_____

Expansion Activity
This, That, These, and Those—
Yes-No Questions

Name _____ Date _____

A Will and his sister Anna are cleaning the living room. They are with their mother. Read the conversation. Circle the correct choices in parentheses.

Mother: Anna, (is this/are these) your CD?

Anna: No, it's not. It's his CD.

Mother: Will, (is that/are those) your books over there?

Will: The red book is my book. The green book is her book.

Mother: Anna, (is this/are these) your clothes?

Anna: These are my shoes. This is his shirt.

Will: And these are my jeans.

Mother: Will, (is this/are these) your toys?

Will: No, they aren't. They're her toys.

Mother: Anna, (is that/are those) your watch?

Anna: Yes, it is.

Mother: Will, (is this/are these) your ribbon?

Will: No way! That's her ribbon.

B Look at the nouns below. Write each noun in the correct box. Use the information from Exercise A.

~~toys~~	watch	shirt	jeans	ribbon
the green book	CD	the red book	shoes	

Anna	Will
toys	

Expansion Activity
This, That, These, and Those—
Questions With *What*

Name _____ Date _____

A Write questions and answers for the underlined nouns in each sentence.

1. There is a <u>statue</u> across the street.

   _____ *What's that?* _____

   _____ *It's a statue.* _____

2. There are <u>some shoes</u> near you.

   _____

   _____

3. You are next to <u>a computer</u>.

   _____

   _____

4. There is <u>a library</u> one block away.

   _____

   _____

5. There are <u>telephones</u> across the room.

   _____

   _____

6. There is <u>a school</u> across the street.

   _____

   _____

7. There are <u>entertainers</u> down the street.

   _____

   _____

8. Two <u>headphones</u> are in your hand.

   _____

   _____

9. You are in <u>a mall</u>.

   _____

   _____

LESSON

17

Expansion Activity
Questions with *What's*

Name _____ Date _____

A Read the conversation. Anna and Helen are in the park with their children.
Underline *What's*.

Anna: That's my son.
Helen: <u>What's</u> his name?
Anna: His name is Tom.
Helen: That's a nice name. What's his middle name?
Anna: It's Robert.
Helen: That's my daughter.
Anna: What's her name?
Helen: Robin.
Anna: What's her middle name?
Helen: Maria. We live in that house over there.
Anna: Is it the pink house?
Helen: No, it's blue.
Anna: What's the address?
Helen: It's 1411 Pine Street.
Anna: Really! We live near you. We're in that house over there.
Helen: Is it the brown house?
Anna: Yes, that's it.
Helen: What's the address?
Anna: It's 1415 Pine Street.
Helen: We're neighbors! What's your phone number?
Anna: It's 555-2579. What's your phone number?
Helen: It's 555-9752. Please call me.

B Complete the chart. Use the information in Exercise A.

Tom	Robin
Middle Name: *Robert*	Middle Name:
Address:	Address:
House Color:	House Color:
Telephone Number:	Telephone Number:

Expansion Activity
Questions with *Where*

Name _____ Date _____

A Put the words in the correct order to make questions with *Where*.

1. is/the Eiffel Tower/Where

   <u>Where is the Eiffel Tower?</u> _____

2. Where/the Alps/are

   _____

3. is/the Great Wall/Where

   _____

4. is/Where/the Amazon River

   _____

5. Where/is/Stonehenge

   _____

6. the Ural Mountains/Where/are

   _____

7. is/Where/the Statue of Liberty

   _____

8. is/the Golden Gate Bridge/Where

   _____

9. Where/the Pyramids/are

   _____

10. is/Hollywood/Where

    _____

B Work with a partner. Write answers to the questions in Exercise A on a separate piece of paper.

EXAMPLE: 1. It's in Paris, France.

Expansion Activity
Questions with *Where* and *What*

Name _____ Date _____

A Fill in the chart below with the following words.

American	Spanish	Japanese	Chinese
French	English	Vietnamese	Brazil
Mexican	France	Japan	
Vietnam	Portuguese	China	

Name	Country	Nationality	First Language
Akiko		Japanese	Japanese
Maria	Mexico		
Nguyen		Vietnamese	
Pierre			French
Andy	United States		
Antonio		Brazilian	
Lee			Chinese

B Answer the questions. Use the information in Exercise A.

1. **Nguyen**
Where is he from?   He's from Vietnam. _____

2. **Andy**
What's his first language?   _____

3. **Pierre**
What's his nationality?   _____

4. **Antonio**
Where is he from?   _____

5. **Lee**
Where is she from?   _____

6. **Maria**
What is her first language? _____

7. **Akiko**
What is her nationality?   _____

Expansion Activity
Questions with *When* and *What time* (Prepositions)

Name _____ Date _____

A Put the words in the correct order to make questions. Then answer the questions. Use the information in Anna's schedule.

Anna's schedule:

Sunday	Monday	Tuesday	Wednesday	Thursday	Friday	Saturday
Basketball game	English class—1:00	English class—1:00	English class—1:00 My birthday party—6:00	English class—1:00	Appointment with Peter —10:00 English class—1:00	Picnic in the park

1. time/is/English class/What/her

Q: *What time is her English class?*

A: *It's at 1:00*

2. basketball game/is/When/the

Q: _____

A: _____

3. is/in the park/the picnic/When

Q: _____

A: _____

4. her/time/birthday party/What/is

Q: _____

A: _____

5. time/appointment with Peter/her/What/is

Q: _____

A: _____

Expansion Activity
Questions with *How is* and *How are* (Adjectives)

Name _____ Date _____

A Put a check next to the correct answer.

1. How's the weather?

✔ It's sunny.

_____ Yes, it is.

_____ They're sunny.

2. How is work?

_____ It's windy.

_____ I'm fine.

_____ It's busy.

3. How are your pancakes?

_____ It's cold.

_____ They're cold.

_____ Yes, they are.

4. How's your soup?

_____ It's not very good.

_____ I'm not very good.

_____ Yes, it is.

5. How are you?

_____ It's fine.

_____ I'm fine.

_____ No, I'm not.

6. How's the beach?

_____ It's beautiful!

_____ Yes, it is.

_____ I'm fine.

7. How are your kids?

_____ We're great.

_____ It's great.

_____ They're great.

8. How is your mother?

_____ I'm fine.

_____ She's fine.

_____ He's fine.

B Write four more questions with *How is* or *How are*.

1. _____

2. _____

3. _____

4. _____

Expansion Activity

Demonstrative Adjectives *This, That, These,* and *Those*

Name _____ Date _____

A Fill in the blanks with *this, that, these,* or *those*.

1. There are expensive shoes near you.

   _____These_____ shoes are expensive.

2. You are next to a new computer.

   _____ computer is new.

3. There is a large library one block away.

   _____ library is large.

4. There are unfriendly customers across the room.

   _____ customers are unfriendly.

5. There is an old school across the street.

   _____ school is old.

6. There are cheap T-shirts over there.

   _____ T-shirts are cheap.

7. Two nice glasses are on a table in front of you.

   _____ glasses are nice.

8. You are in a crowded store.

   _____ store is crowded.

Expansion Activity
Questions with *How much* and *How old*

Name _____ Date _____

A Complete the first line of the chart. Then ask five of your classmates the question. Complete the chart. Use complete sentences.

How old are you?

Name	Age
You	I am _____ years old.

B Answer questions for the city where you live. Use the word *about* in your answers.

EXAMPLE: Q: How much is a hamburger?

A: It's about $1.50.

1. How much are shoes?

A: _____

2. How much is a sandwich?

A: _____

3. How much is a movie?

A: _____

4. How much are pants?

A: _____

5. How much is a notebook?

A: _____

Expansion Activity
Questions with *Who*

Name _____ Date _____

A Read the paragraph. Circle the nouns. Underline the adjectives.

My Brother and Sister and Me

My (name) is (Jose) I'm a (student) I'm <u>single</u>. I am always busy at school. My sister Maria is an architect. She is always busy. She is very hardworking. Her office is in a tall building. She is single. My brother Mario is a teacher. He is funny and friendly. He is a good cook. He is married. Helen is his wife. We are all from San Francisco. I love my family.

B Read the questions. Check the correct boxes.

	Jose	**Maria**	**Mario**
1. Who's a student?			
2. Who's single?	✓		
3. Who's an architect?			
4. Who's a good cook?			
5. Who's from San Francisco?			
6. Who's friendly?			
7. Who is hardworking?			
8. Who's always busy?			

Expansion Activity
Questions with *When, What time,* and *How long*

Name _____ Date _____

A Read the questions below. Check the best answers.

1. When is her birthday?

_____ It's from 6:00 to 8:00.

_____ It's around two hours long.

_____ It's in February.

2. What time is your class?

_____ It's at 3:00.

_____ It's around two hours long.

_____ It's on Monday.

3. How long is the movie?

_____ It's at 5:00.

_____ It's around two hours long.

_____ It's on Wednesday.

B Write *true* answers for the questions below. Then write three more questions and true answers.

1. What time is your class?

_____

2. How long is your class?

_____

3. When is Independence Day in the U.S.?

_____

4. What time _____

_____

5. How long _____

_____

6. When _____

_____

Expansion Activity
There/Their/They're

Name _____ Date _____

A Put the words in the correct order to make sentences.

1. over/They/are/there

They are over there.

2. are/their/family/There/two children/in

_____

3. their/are/car/They/in

_____

4. father/over/Their/there/is

_____

5. mother/They're/with/their

_____

6. is/monkey/over/there/There/a

_____

7. there/parents/Their/aren't

_____

8. in/house/are/two bedrooms/their/There

_____

9. teacher/their/in/school/They're/their/with

_____

10. there/children/are/Their

_____

Expansion Activity
Possessive Nouns

Name _____ Date _____

A Read the paragraph. Circle the family nouns.

John's Family

John loves his family. Kathy is his (mother.) She is a doctor. His father's name is Joe. He's a lawyer. John's sister is Carol. She's a teacher. John has two brothers, Harry and James. Harry is an architect. James is an artist. John is married. His wife is Sue. Sue is a music teacher. John's son is Martin. Martin is a student. John's family is very big!

B Fill in each blank with a possessive name. Use the information from Exercise A

EXAMPLE: Joe is _____*John's*_____ father.

1. John is _____ husband.

2. Kathy is _____ grandmother.

3. Harry is _____ brother-in-law.

4. Harry is _____ brother.

5. James is _____ uncle.

6. Martin is _____ grandson.

7. Carol is _____ aunt.

C Fill in each blank with a family word.

1. Harry is Martin's _uncle_____.

2. Martin is Carol's _____.

3. James is Sue's _____.

4. Carol is John's _____.

5. Joe is Martin's _____.

6. Martin is John's _____.

7. Martin is Kathy's _____.

8. Joes is Kathy's _____.

Expansion Activity
Possessive *'s*, Contracted *'s*, and Plural *s*

Name _____ Date _____

A Read the paragraph. Circle all the words that end in possessive *'s*, contracted *'s*, or plural *s*.

(John's) house is very big. There are three bedrooms and two bathrooms. John's in the house now. He's in the living room. There's a party right now. John's friends are at the party. John's happy. His friends are happy, too.

B Use the circled words from Exercise A to complete the chart below.

Possessive *'s*	Contracted *'s*	Plural *s*
John's		

LESSON 29

Expansion Activity
Present Tense of GO

Name _____ Date _____

A Read the paragraphs. Underline the word *goes*.

Robert is a student. Every weekday, he <u>goes</u> to school at 9:00. He goes home at 5:00. He goes to bed around 11:00. On weekends, he often goes to the beach. Every summer, he goes to the mountains.

Karen is an architect. Her office is in a tall building. Her building is downtown. Every weekday, she goes to work at 8:00 a.m. She goes home around 6:00. On Saturdays, she goes to the beach. On Sundays, she goes to the mall. Sometimes, she goes to the movies.

Andy is a doctor. His office is downtown. He always goes to work at 9:00 a.m. On Mondays and Wednesdays, he goes home at 4:00. On Tuesdays, Thursdays, and Fridays, he goes home at 7:00. He goes to bed at 10:00. Every Saturday, he goes to the movies.

B Read the sentences. Check the correct boxes.

He or She...	Robert	Karen	Andy
...goes to school.	✓		
...goes downtown to work.			
...goes to work at 9:00.			
...goes to the beach.			
...goes home at 5:00.			
...goes to the mall on Sundays.			
...goes to the movies on Saturdays.			
...goes to the mountains every summer.			
...sometimes goes home at 4:00.			

Expansion Activity

Present Tense of GO + Activities
(*go* ___ *ing*)
_{verb}

Name _____ Date _____

A Circle your eight favorite activities.

go skiing	go shopping	go dancing	go swimming
go bike-riding	go jogging	go ice-skating	go sightseeing
go to the mountains	go to the beach	go to the mall	go to a new place
go to the movies	go to the park	go to the zoo	go to school

B Write sentences with the activities you circled above. Use time words like *every weekend* and *in the summer*.

EXAMPLE: *I go to the mountains every spring* _____

1. _____

2. _____

3. _____

4. _____

5. _____

5. _____

6. _____

7. _____

8. _____

Expansion Activity
Present Tense—Affirmative Statements

Name _____ Date _____

A Read the paragraph. Underline the verbs in the present tense.

Ann and Kim

Ann and Kim <u>are</u> sisters. Ann <u>gets up</u> at 6:00 every day. Kim gets up at 10:00. Ann takes a shower in the morning. Kim takes a shower every night. Ann teaches children at a school. She works from 8:00 to 4:00. Kim works in a restaurant. She's a waitress. She works from 3:00 to 11:00. On weekends, Ann rides her bike in the mountains. Kim goes shopping at the mall. Ann and Kim are very different.

B Circle the correct name. Use the information in Exercise A

1. (Ann/Kim) gets up at 10:00.

2. (Ann/Kim) goes shopping at the mall on weekends.

3. (Ann/Kim) takes a shower in the morning.

4. (Ann/Kim) works from 8:00 to 4:00.

5. (Ann/Kim) works in a restaurant.

C Fill in each blank below with the correct form of a verb from the list below.

ride   get up   take   go
brush   eat

1. I _____eat_____ breakfast at 8:00.

2. She _____ her bike on Saturdays.

3. We _____ dancing once a week.

4. He _____ a shower in the morning.

5. The children _____ their teeth at night.

6. Jack _____ late on Sundays.

Expansion Activity
Present Tense—Spelling

Name _____ Date _____

A Write the present tense *he/she* forms of the verbs.

1. carry   _carries_____

2. work   _____

3. fix   _____

4. wake up   _____

5. go   _____

6. eat   _____

7. brush   _____

8. get   _____

9. play   _____

10. live   _____

11. try   _____

12. write   _____

13. wash   _____

14. make   _____

15. watch   _____

16. take   _____

17. miss   _____

18. drink   _____

B **Spelling Bee** Stand in a line. Your teacher will say a verb in the base form. One by one, students will spell the present tense forms. When students make mistakes, they will sit down. The last student spelling a verb correctly is the winner.

Expansion Activity
Present Tense of *Do*, *Have*, *Make*, and *Take*—Affirmative Statements

Name _____ Date _____

A Work with a partner. Read the questions to your partner. Write your partner's answers.

> ### *My partner,*
> _____
> (your partner's first name)
>
> | **Questions** | **Your Partner's Answers** |
> |---|---|
> | 1. Who makes dinner in your house? | _____ |
> | 2. Who does the laundry? | _____ |
> | 3. Who takes a bus in your family? | _____ |
> | 4. Who makes your bed? | _____ |
> | 5. Who does the dishes in your house? | _____ |
> | 6. Who has breakfast in your house? | _____ |
> | 7. Who has a job in your family? | _____ |

B Write five sentences about your partner.

EXAMPLE: *Maria's father makes dinner in her house.*

1. _____

2. _____

3. _____

4. _____

5. _____

Expansion Activity
Present Tense—Negative Statements

Name _____ Date _____

A Circle the correct form of the verb in each sentence.

1. Jane (works/work) in a computer company.

2. She (gets up/get up) at 6:00 in the morning.

3. She (don't eat/doesn't eat) breakfast at home.

4. She (don't drive/doesn't drive) to work.

5. She (takes/take) the bus.

6. She (don't go/doesn't go) to her office every day.

7. She (goes/go) to Sandy's house every Saturday for lunch.

8. They (doesn't eat/don't eat) lunch at Sandy's house.

9. They (go/goes) to a restaurant.

10. After lunch, they (doesn't go/don't go) home.

11. They (take/takes) a walk in the park.

12. After their walk, they (go/goes) back to Sandy's house.

13. They (play/plays) music together.

14. Sandy (plays/play) the piano.

15. Jane (don't play/doesn't play) the piano.

B Circle the choice that makes each sentence *true* about you.

1. I (play/don't play) the piano.

2. I (go/don't go) to school every weekday.

3. I (use/don't use) a computer every day.

4. I (have/don't have) a dog.

5. I (watch/don't watch) TV a lot.

Expansion Activity
Present Tense—Yes-No Questions and Short Answers

Name _____ Date _____

A For each affirmative statement, write a negative statement and a yes-no question.

1. Ben teaches third grade.

    Ben doesn't teach third grade.

    Does Ben teach third grade?

2. It rains in April.

    _____

    _____

3. They want pizza.

    _____

    _____

4. Carolyn likes singing.

    _____

    _____

5. You go to the beach on weekends.

    _____

    _____

6. I'm late for class.

    _____

    _____

Expansion Activity
Present Tense with Frequency Adverbs

Name _____ Date _____

A Put the words in the correct order to make sentences.

1. *always / tennis / I / play / on Saturdays*

   <u>I always play tennis on Saturdays.</u>

2. in the summer/swimming/often/go/We

   _____

3. plays/in the winter/She/rarely/baseball

   _____

4. for work/usually/Steve/late/is

   _____

5. go/sometimes/on weekends/They/to the beach

   _____

6. on weekdays/He/to school/goes/always

   _____

7. go/with John/I/skiing/never

   _____

Expansion Activity
Present Tense of *Want, Need, Like,* and *Have* + Infinitives

Name _____ Date _____

A Read the paragraph. Underline all forms of *want, need, like,* and *have +
infinitive.*

Maria's Life

Maria is a college student in New York City. She goes to class from
Monday to Friday. She <u>has to take</u> the bus. Her classes are very difficult.
She needs to study every day. On the weekends, Maria has to work in a
restaurant. She doesn't like to work there. She needs to get money for
school. In the summer, Maria takes a short vacation. She likes to go to
the beach. She likes to swim. In the winter, she likes to go to the mountains. She doesn't like to ski. She goes ice-skating. After college, Maria
wants to be an architect. She wants to work in Mexico City or Los
Angeles. It's warm there. She doesn't want to stay in New York. It's very
cold there.

B Fill in each blank with *true* or *false.* Use the information in Exercise A.

EXAMPLE:
_____true_____ Maria is a college student.

1. _____ Maria needs to study every day.

2. _____ Maria likes to ski in the winter.

3. _____ Maria wants to work in New York City after college.

4. _____ Maria likes the weather in Mexico City and Los Angeles.

5. _____ Maria drives her car to school.

6. _____ Maria doesn't like to go to the beach.

7. _____ Maria sometimes goes ice-skating in the winter.

8. _____ Maria is very rich.

9. _____ Maria doesn't want to be a waitress after college.

10. _____ Maria's classes aren't easy.

Expansion Activity
Present Tense—Questions with
What/Where/When/Why/Who

Name _____ Date _____

A Put the words in the correct order to make sentences.

1. you/do/on/weekends/What/do

   What do you do on weekends? _____

2. go/I/the/beach/to

   _____

3. he/does/go/Where/to/school

   _____

4. to/in Chicago/ school/goes/He

   _____

5. does/have/Why/two jobs/he

   _____

6. to/He/his family/money/sends

   _____

B Write a *Wh* question for each answer. Use the question word in parentheses.

1. (What time) _What time does the movie start?_ _____

   The movie starts at 7:00.

2. (What) _____

   On weekends, she goes swimming.

3. (Who) _____

   I work with Maria, Henry, and Paul.

4. (Where) _____

   They go to the mountains in the winter.

5. (When) _____

   My English course begins on September 3.

6. (What time) _____

   They eat dinner at 6:00.

LESSON 39

Expansion Activity

Present Continuous Tense— Affirmative Statements

Name _____ Date _____

A Look around your class. What are the people doing? Write eight sentences about the students and your teacher. Then read your sentences to a partner.

EXAMPLE: ____*Maria is talking to the teacher.*_____

1. _____

2. _____

3. _____

4. _____

5. _____

6. _____

7. _____

8. _____

B **Guessing Game** Find two partners. Act out actions. Guess the actions.

EXAMPLE:

Partner 1 :   *You're walking.*

You :   *No, that's not right.*

Partner 2 :   *You're running.*

You :   *Yes, that's right.*

Expansion Activity
Present Continuous Tense—Spelling

Name _____ Date _____

A Write the verbs in the *-ing* form.

1. put   *putting* _____

2. read   _____

3. stop   _____

4. listen   _____

5. have   _____

6. carry   _____

7. eat   _____

8. cry   _____

9. stand   _____

10. sit   _____

11. write   _____

12. rain   _____

13. walk   _____

14. work   _____

15. give   _____

16. sleep   _____

17. run   _____

18. dance   _____

B **Spelling Bee** Stand in a line. Your teacher will say a verb in the base form. One by one, students will spell the present continuous tense forms. When students make mistakes, they will sit down. The last student spelling a verb correctly is the winner.

Expansion Activity
Present Continuous Tense—Negative Statements

Name _____ Date _____

A For each affirmative statement, write a negative statement.

1. They are eating breakfast.

   *They aren't eating breakfast.* OR *They're not eating breakfast.*

2. She's reading a magazine.

   _____

3. They're taking a walk in the park.

   _____

4. We're playing cards.

   _____

5. It's sitting in the tree.

   _____

6. I'm eating dinner with my friends.

   _____

7. You're standing on my foot.

   _____

8. Lou is writing a letter.

   _____

9. It's snowing in the mountains.

   _____

10. Mike and Thomas are carrying my luggage.

   _____

Expansion Activity
Present Continuous Tense—Yes-No Questions and Short Answers

Name _____ Date _____

A Look around your class. What are the people doing? Write five yes-no questions about the students and your teacher. The questions can be funny or serious.

EXAMPLE: *Are the students reading?*

 Is the teacher playing basketball?

1. _____

2. _____

3. _____

4. _____

5. _____

B Find a partner. Read your questions. Write your partner's answers. Then answer your partner's questions.

1. _____

2. _____

3. _____

4. _____

5. _____

Expansion Activity

Present Continuous Tense—*Wh* Questions and Short Answers

Name _____ Date _____

A Read the *Wh* questions below. Write two new questions for your classmates.

1. How are you doing?

2. What are you doing?

3. What is the teacher doing?

4. Why are you studying English?

5. What are you doing after this class?

6. What time are you going home today?

7. _____

8. _____

B Walk around the room. Ask different students your questions. Answer their questions.

C Put the words in the correct order to make *Wh* questions.

1. cooking/you/are/What

_____

2. are/we/When/going/home

_____

3. to the party/coming/Who/is

_____

4. is/leaving/he/Why

_____

5. your/is/going/brother/Where

_____

Expansion Activity

Contrast: Present and Present Continuous Tenses

Name _____ Date _____

A Read the questions below. Write three new questions. Write two questions in the present tense and one question in the present continuous tense.

1. How are you doing?

2. What do you like to do in the summer?

3. Are you going to the movies tonight?

4. What do you do on Saturdays?

5. What are you doing after this class?

6. _____

7. _____

8. _____

B Answer the questions from Exercise A.

1. _____

2. _____

3. _____

4. _____

5. _____

6. _____

7. _____

8. _____

Expansion Activity

Contrast: *BE* and *DO* in Present Tense Negative Statements and Questions

Name _____ Date _____

A For each affirmative statement, write a negative statement and a yes-no question.

EXAMPLE:

1. Ann eats breakfast at 8:00 every morning.

   Ann doesn't eat breakfast at 8:00 every morning.

   Does Ann eat breakfast at 8:00 every morning?

2. They go to the mountains in the summer.

   _____

   _____

3. He's doing the laundry.

   _____

   _____

4. She's very friendly.

   _____

   _____

5. You visit your parents in the winter.

   _____

   _____

6. We're from San Francisco.

   _____

   _____

7. He wants to take a vacation.

   _____

   _____

Expansion Activity

CAN—Affirmative and Negative Statements

Name _____ Date _____

A Change the sentences to *can* sentences.

EXAMPLE:　Sue doesn't play the piano.　Sue cooks pizza.

<u>Sue can't play the piano.</u>　<u>Sue can cook pizza.</u>

1. John speaks English very well.

_____

2. Mary doesn't swim.

_____

3. We speak Chinese and French.

_____

4. They don't play the piano.

_____

5. I play basketball.

_____

6. I don't play volleyball.

_____

7. She doesn't read English.

_____

8. They swim and they fly kites.

_____

9. He speaks Chinese, but he doesn't speak Japanese.

_____

10. We don't go to the mountains in the summer.

_____

Expansion Activity
CAN—Yes-No Questions and Short Answers

Name _____ Date _____

A Read the paragraph. Then read the questions below and circle the correct answers.

Helen and Mike

Helen and Mike are married. They live in Chicago. Helen is from France. She speaks French and English. Her mother is from Spain, but Helen doesn't speak Spanish. Mike speaks only English. They are teachers. Helen teaches music. She plays the piano and the guitar, but she doesn't play the drums. Mike teaches computer classes. After school, they go home. Sometimes Helen cooks dinner. Sometimes Mike cooks dinner. On weekends, they like to go to the beach. They swim in the lake. Helen likes sailing, but Mike can't sail. He likes to go surfing. Helen doesn't surf. In the winter, they go to the mountains. They often go skiing, but they can't ice-skate. They have a good life!

1. Can Mike speak French?	Yes, he can.	No, he can't.
2. Can Mike and Helen speak English?	Yes, they can.	No, they can't.
3. Can Helen speak Spanish?	Yes, she can.	No, she can't.
4. Can Helen and Mike swim?	Yes, they can.	No, they can't.
5. Can Helen sail?	Yes, she can.	No, she can't.
6. Can Helen and Mike ice-skate?	Yes, they can.	No, they can't.
7. Can Mike surf?	Yes, he can.	No, he can't.
8. Can Helen and Mike ski?	Yes, they can.	No, they can't.
9. Can Mike sail?	Yes, he can.	No, he can't.
10. Can Helen surf?	Yes, she can.	No, she can't.
11. Can Helen play the piano?	Yes, she can.	No, she can't.
12. Can Helen play the drums?	Yes, she can.	No, she can't.

Expansion Activity

Past Tense of *BE*—Affirmative and Negative Statements

Name _____ Date _____

A Fill in each blank with *was* or *were*.

1. We _____ were _____ in Europe a year ago.

2. Yesterday, she _____ at school.

3. The waiter _____ very busy last night.

4. They _____ in Hawaii last week.

5. I _____ busy last year.

6. There _____ flowers on the table.

7. I _____ at the beach yesterday.

8. My sister _____ here last week.

B Fill in each blank with *wasn't* or *weren't*.

1. I _____ home yesterday.

2. They _____ there two years ago.

3. The restaurant _____ crowded.

4. Susan _____ in the living room.

5. You _____ in class last week.

6. We _____ at home last night.

7. It _____ very expensive.

8. My brother and sister _____ here yesterday.

LESSON 49

Expansion Activity
Past Tense of *BE*—Yes-No Questions and Short Answers

Name _____ Date _____

A Look at the questions. Write your answers.

EXAMPLE: Were you at school yesterday? *Yes, I was.* OR *No, I wasn't.*

Questions	Me
1. Were you at school yesterday?	
2. One year ago, were you a student?	
3. Were you married or single last year?	
4. Were you at home last night?	
5. Were you happy or sad yesterday?	
6. Was your birthday last month?	
7. Were you busy last week?	

B Find a partner. Ask your partner the questions. Write answers with *he* or *she*.

EXAMPLE: Were you at school yesterday? *Yes, she was.* OR *No, she wasn't.*

Questions	My Partner
1. Were you at school yesterday?	
2. One year ago, were you a student?	
3. Were you married or single last year?	
4. Were you at home last night?	
5. Were you happy or sad yesterday?	
6. Was your birthday last month?	
7. Were you busy last week?	

Expansion Activity
Past Tense of *BE*—*Wh* Questions and Short Answers

Name _____ Date _____

A Match each question with the correct answer.

1. __j__ Were you in Japan last year?   a. It was Robert.

2. _____ How much were those shoes?   b. It was last Thursday.

3. _____ What was his name?   c. Because I was sick.

4. _____ How old was their son?   d. It was at 8:30.

5. _____ Why were you absent?   e. They were $40.00.

6. _____ Who was sick yesterday?   f. Yes, there were.

7. _____ Was this book interesting?   g. It was three hours long.

8. _____ When was her birthday?   h. He was thirteen years old.

9. _____ What time was the movie?   i. Helen, Ann, and Joe were.

10. _____ Were there monkeys at the zoo?   j. Yes, I was.

11. _____ How long was the play?   k. Yes, it was.

12. _____ Where were you born?   l. In China.

Expansion Activity

Contrast: Past and Present Tenses of *BE*

Name _____ Date _____

A Read the questions below. Write four new questions. Write two questions in the present tense and two questions in the past tense.

1. Were you busy yesterday?

2. Are you busy today?

3. Are you a student now?

4. Were you a student last year?

5. Where were you last night?

6. Where are you now?

7. _____

8. _____

9. _____

10. _____

B Answer the questions from Exercise A.

1. _____

2. _____

3. _____

4. _____

5. _____

6. _____

7. _____

8. _____

9. _____

10. _____

Expansion Activity

Past Tense—Affirmative Statements

Name _____ Date _____

A Write the following expressions in the calendar below. Pretend that today is Thursday, May 13.

~~today~~   the day before yesterday   three days ago
last weekend   yesterday   last Thursday

May					
Saturday and Sunday	**Monday**	**Tuesday**	**Wednesday**	**Thursday**	**Friday**
1/2	3	4	5	6	7
8/9	10	11	12	13 today	14

B Complete each sentence with *true* information. Then read your sentences to a partner.

EXAMPLE: Last year, I _____ visited friends in Texas. _____

1. Yesterday, I _____

2. The day before yesterday, I _____

3. Three days ago, I _____

4. Last weekend, I _____

5. Last Thursday, I _____

LESSON

53

Expansion Activity

Past Tense—Spelling and Pronunciation of Regular Verbs

Name _____ Date _____

A Write the past tense forms of the verbs.

1. worry *worried* _____

2. clap _____

3. smile _____

4. stop _____

5. marry _____

6. sip _____

7. play _____

8. talk _____

9. show _____

10. hug _____

11. carry _____

12. fix _____

13. cry _____

14. dance _____

15. need _____

16. want _____

17. rub _____

18. study _____

Expansion Activity
Past Tense—Irregular Verbs

Name _____ Date _____

A Read the paragraph. Underline all of the past tense verbs.

John's Day

Yesterday, John <u>got up</u> at 8:00. He took a shower. Then he ate breakfast. He left his house at 8:45. He got in his car and drove to work. He works in an office downtown. He is an architect. John worked all day. After work, he went to a Mexican restaurant for dinner. Then he went to a movie. He got home around 10:00 and went to bed.

B Write a paragraph about your day yesterday. What did you do?

My Day

_____ *Yesterday, I* _____

_____

_____

_____

_____

_____

_____

_____

_____

_____

_____

LESSON 55

Expansion Activity

Past Tense—Negative Statements

Name _____ Date _____

A For each affirmative statement, write a negative statement.

1. I got up early yesterday.

  I didn't get up early yesterday. _____

2. It rained last night.

  _____

3. They made dinner.

  _____

4. We went to the movies.

  _____

5. Jack called me on Saturday.

  _____

6. You gave me ride yesterday.

  _____

B Write four sentences about things you didn't do. Use the words in parentheses.

EXAMPLE: (this morning) _____ _I didn't get up early this morning._ _____

1. (this morning) _____

2. (yesterday) _____

3. (last night) _____

4. (on Tuesday) _____

5. (two days ago) _____

Expansion Activity

Contrast: *BE* and *DO* in Past Tense Negative Statements

Name _____ Date _____

A Read the paragraph. Underline all of the past tense verbs.

Last Weekend

Judy, Andy, and Mika <u>did</u> a lot last weekend. On Saturday morning, Judy went shopping with Mika. Andy didn't go shopping. He was at the beach. He swam for one hour. They all met for lunch at a nice restaurant. In the afternoon, Judy went home and studied. Andy and Mika were downtown. They saw a movie. Andy didn't like it. At night, Andy and Judy went dancing. Mika stayed home and watched TV. Everyone slept late on Sunday. Andy and Mika made a delicious breakfast. Then Mika and Judy went to the park. They played tennis for two hours. Andy didn't want to play tennis. He walked to the supermarket and bought groceries. Later, he cooked dinner for Mika and Judy. At night, Mika, Judy, and Andy were at home. Mika and Judy were tired from tennis. They went to bed at 9:00. Andy wasn't tired. He watched TV until 11:00. It was a busy weekend!

B Read the sentences. Check the correct boxes.

Who...	Judy	Mika	Andy
...didn't go shopping on Saturday?			✓
...wasn't at the beach?			
...went to a movie?			
...didn't like the movie?			
...wasn't downtown Saturday afternoon?			
...didn't go dancing?			
...slept late on Sunday?			
...didn't play tennis?			
...was at home Sunday night?			
...wasn't tired Sunday night?			

Expansion Activity

Contrast: *BE* and *DO* Past Tense
Yes-No Questions and Answers

Name _____ Date _____

A For each affirmative statement, write a yes-no question.

1. You went to New York last year.

   Did you go to New York last year?

2. You took the bus to school yesterday.

   _____

3. It was very cold.

   _____

4. She came to my house this morning.

   _____

5. You were a student two years ago.

   _____

6. They were at the beach yesterday.

   _____

7. I ate dinner at my friend's house last night.

   _____

8. We went skiing in Colorado last year.

   _____

9. She made a salad for the party.

   _____

10. There were five students in the class.

    _____

11. We heard a lot of beautiful music at the concert.

    _____

Expansion Activity
Past Tense: *Wh* Questions and Short Answers

Name _____ Date _____

A Match each question with the correct answer.

1. ___h___ How much did you pay for it?
2. _____ What did you do yesterday?
3. _____ Was it a good movie?
4. _____ How did she get there?
5. _____ Were there many people there?
6. _____ Where did he go?
7. _____ When did he go to Mexico?
8. _____ Who did they meet?
9. _____ What time did you leave?
10. _____ Why did you study for six hours?
11. _____ How long was the play?

a. Yes, there were.
b. At 9:00.
c. I watched TV all day.
d. Martin and Helen.
e. Yes, it was.
f. Last year
g. To the beach.
h. It was $15.00.
i. By bus.
j. It was three hours long.
k. Because I had a big test.

B Fill in each blank with *in, on, at, because, by,* or *to.*

1. He worked two jobs _____because_____ he needed money.

2. Her birthday was _____ February.

3. We went to the movie _____ Saturday.

4. They traveled _____ plane.

5. They got home _____ 10:00.

6. We went _____ the mountains last December.

LESSON 59

Expansion Activity

Contrast: *BE* and *DO* in Past Tense Questions and Answers

Name _____ Date _____

A For each affirmative statement, write a yes-no question.

1. I went to the beach yesterday.

   Did you go to the beach yesterday? _____

2. She was very happy in Beijing.

   _____

3. He went to the beach yesterday.

   _____

4. They ate dinner at a restaurant last night.

   _____

5. Henry and Anna wanted to see us.

   _____

B Write a *Wh* question for each answer. Use the question word in parentheses.

1. (where)_____
I lived in Guatemala last year.

2. (how)_____
I went to school by bus.

3. (why)_____
He was in China because his family lives there.

4. (where)_____
She studied in the library.

5. (who)_____
Kevin married Jane.

6. (when)_____
They saw the movie last night.

Expansion Activity

Contrast Three Verb Tenses: Present, Present Continuous, and Past

Name _____ Date _____

A Read about Ricky again on page 176 of your book. Write a similar story about your life. Answer these questions:

- Where did you live? Who did you live with? What was your childhood like?

- What is your life like now? What do you do every day? What do you do on weekends?

- Where are you now? What are you doing? What are you thinking about?

My Life

_____

_____

_____

_____

_____

_____

_____

_____

_____

_____

_____

_____

_____

_____

Now read your story to a partner.

LESSON 61

Expansion Activity

Future Tense with *Be going to*— Affirmative Statements

Name _____ Date _____

A Fill in the blanks with *am/is/are going to* + the verbs in parentheses.

1. I (go) *'m going to go* _____ to my friend's house tonight.

2. Marion (stay) _____ at our house.

3. Joe and Ella (cook) _____ dinner for us.

4. You (be) _____ late for school.

5. Janet and I (have) _____ lunch together tomorrow.

6. Ed (buy) _____ a new car next year.

B Complete the sentences below with *true* information about your life. Use the future tense with *be going to*.

1. On Monday, *I'm going to go to the movies.* _____

2. On Saturday, _____

3. This week, _____

4. Next week, _____

5. Tomorrow, _____

6. The day after tomorrow, _____

7. Next month, _____

8. Next year, _____

9. In a little while, _____

10. In four days, _____

Expansion Activity

Future Tense with *Be going to*— Negative Statements

Name _____ Date _____

A Write each of the following expressions in the calendar below. Pretend today is Tuesday, May 4.

~~today~~   the day after tomorrow   in three days
next weekend   tomorrow   next Monday

May					
Saturday and Sunday	**Monday**	**Tuesday**	**Wednesday**	**Thursday**	**Friday**
1/2	3	4 *today*	5	6	7
8/9	10	11	12	13	14

B Complete the sentences with *true* information. Write negative sentences.

EXAMPLE: Tomorrow, *I'm not going to be with my family.*

1. Tomorrow, _____

2. The day after tomorrow, _____

3. Next weekend, _____

4. In three days, _____

5. Next month, _____

6. Next year, _____

Expansion Activity

Future Tense with *Be going to*—
Yes-No Questions and Short Answers

Name _____ Date _____

A Read the questions. Write three new questions.

1. Are you going to see a movie next weekend?

2. Are you going to take a bus this week?

3. Are you going to go to school tomorrow?

4. Is it going to rain tomorrow?

5. Is it going to be warm tomorrow?

6. _____

7. _____

8. _____

B Write answers to the questions in Exercise A.

1. _____

2. _____

3. _____

4. _____

5. _____

6. _____

7. _____

8. _____

Expansion Activity

Future Tense with *Be going to*—*Wh* Questions and Short Answers

Name _____ Date _____

A Write a *Wh* question for each answer. Use the question word in parentheses.

1. (what time) <u>What time is the movie going to start?</u>
The movie is going to start at 8:00.

2. (who) _____
They are going to go to New York with Mary.

3. (why) _____
She is going to study education because she wants to be a teacher.

4. (where) _____
He is going to eat dinner at a nice restaurant.

5. (how) _____
She is going to get here by plane.

6. (when) _____
They are going to go to Europe next month.

7. (what) _____
I'm going to eat a big salad for dinner.

8. how much) _____
The trip is going to cost $1,200.

9. (how long) _____
We are going to be in Europe for two weeks.

10. (what) _____
I'm going to relax this summer.

11. (what time) _____
They're going to be home around 10:00.

Review Test: Lessons 1–4

Name _____ Date _____

A Fill in each blank with *a* or *an*.

1. __a__ book   2. _____ apartment   3. _____ table

4. _____ mother   5. _____ old man   6. _____ house

B Write the subject pronoun in the blank for each word or phrase.

EXAMPLE: *New York* = ___it___

1. Anna and I = _____

2. Disneyland™ = _____

3. Helen and David = _____

4.    = _____

5.    = _____

C Fill in each blank with the correct adjective.

EXAMPLE: (happy, old) __happy__ baby

1. (expensive, old) _____ man

2. (new, sad) _____ table

3. (black, happy) _____ car

4. (sad, big) _____ house

5. (small, happy) _____ city

D Underline the verb in each sentence.

EXAMPLE: On Mondays, I <u>clean</u> my room.

1. On Saturdays, I swim.

2. I live in New York.

3. For fun, I go to a party.

4. I love Chicago.

5. At school, I study English.

E Find the mistakes. Rewrite the sentences.

EXAMPLE: This is a big houses.

This is a big house.

1. New York is big city.   _____

2. It is a apartment.   _____

3. He is a baby happy.   _____

4. He is old man.   _____

5. I like bigs stores.   _____

Review Test: Lessons 5–8

Name _____ Date _____

A Fill in each blank with *am*, *is*, or *are*.

My name ____is____ David. I _____ from Miami.

Helen _____ my wife. We _____ architects. I _____

also a student. Helen _____ the boss in her office. I

_____ not the boss in my office. Helen's office _____

beautiful. Her building _____ downtown. My building

_____ near my school. It _____ not downtown.

B For each affirmative statement, write a negative statement.
EXAMPLE:

He's happy.   ___He's not happy./He isn't happy.___

1. They are married.   _____

2. I am from Chicago.   _____

3. She is beautiful.   _____

4. Mark and I are happy.   _____

5. You are friendly.   _____

C Write new sentences. Use subject pronoun + *BE* (*not*) + adjective + noun.

EXAMPLE:

The store is expensive.   It's *an expensive store.* _____

1. The people are friendly.   They _____

2. The teacher is young.   She _____

3. The children aren't quiet.   They _____

4. The book is cheap.   It _____

5. The jewelry store isn't crowded.   It _____

D Write new sentences. Use the words in parentheses.

EXAMPLE:

Helen is late for work. (always)   *Helen is always late for work.* _____

1. David is home on Saturdays. (never)   _____

2. The children are busy. (usually)   _____

3. Mike and Anna are absent from
   school. (sometimes)   _____

4. Mr. and Mrs. Smith are late. (often)   _____

5. Harry is happy. (always)   _____

Review Test: Lessons 9–11

Name _____ Date _____

A Fill in each blank with *There is* or *There are*.

EXAMPLE: *There are*_____ six books on the table.

1._____people in the class.

2._____a big kitchen in the apartment.

3._____a lot of kids in the neighborhood.

4._____one teacher in my class.

5._____children in the park.

B For each affirmative statement, write a question.

EXAMPLE: *You're very busy.*

_Are you very busy?_____

1. The doctor is a woman.

_____

2. She's at work or at home.

_____

3. There is a big tree in the yard.

_____

4. I'm late.

_____

5. There are parks nearby.

_____

6. He's in the living room.

_____

7. We're on time.

_____

8. There are two teachers in the class.

_____

9. The architect is from Chicago or New York.

_____

10. It's cloudy.

_____

C Read each question. Then check the best answer.

EXAMPLE: Is there a park nearby?

_____Yes, he is.

__✔__ Yes, there is.

_____Yes, I am.

1. Are you a teacher?

_____Yes, you are.

_____Yes, there is.

_____Yes, I am.

2. Is it cloudy?

_____No, it isn't.

_____No, he isn't.

_____No, there isn't.

3. Are you married or single?

_____Yes, you are.

_____I'm married.

_____No, you're not.

4. Is there a mall in this neighborhood?

_____Yes, it is.

_____Yes, there is.

_____Yes, there are.

5. Is he a politician?

_____No, he's not.

_____No, she's not.

_____No, there aren't.

6. Are there schools nearby?

_____Yes, they are.

_____Yes, there are.

_____Yes, there is.

7. Are we in Chicago?

_____No, there aren't.

_____No, they aren't.

_____No, we're not.

8. Is the doctor a man or a woman?

_____Yes, it is.

_____She's a woman.

_____She's at work.

9. Am I late?

_____No, We're not.

_____No, there isn't.

_____No, you're not.

10. Are there two pillows on the bed?

_____Yes, there are.

_____Yes, they are.

_____Yes, there is.

Review Test: Lessons 12–16

Name _____ Date _____

A Read the sentences. Fill in each blank with *This is, That's, These are,* or *Those are.*

EXAMPLE: There is a statue down the street.

That's a statue.

1. You are in front of a building.

_____ a library.

2. There are statues over there in the park.

_____ statues.

3. You have three books in your hands.

_____ my books.

4. You are next to your closet.

_____ my closet.

5. There's a large building down the street.

_____ a school.

6. You are in a park.

_____ a park.

7. A parking lot is one block away.

_____ a parking lot.

8. You are on your bed. You are next to two pillows.

_____ great pillows!

9. You are far from your grandparents.

_____ my grandparents.

10. Your sister is across the room.

_____ my sister.

B For each affirmative statement, write a yes-no question.

EXAMPLE: This is a book.

Is this a book?

1. These are CDs.

_____

2. That's a stereo.

_____

3. Those are her clothes.

_____

4. This is an MP3 player.

_____

5. Those are his chairs.

_____

C Look at each answer. Circle the correct question.

EXAMPLE: Q: (Is this your book?/What's this?)

A: Yes, it's my book.

1. Q: (Is this your book?/Are these your books?)
   A: No, they're not. They're his books.

2. Q: (What are those?/Are those statues?)
   A: Those are statues.

3. Q: (What are these?/What's this?)
   A: They're CDs.

4. Q: (What's this?/Is this your bedroom?)
   A: Yes, it is.

5. Q: (What's that?/What are those?)
   A: That's a stereo.

Review Test: Lessons 17–21

Name _____ Date _____

A Fill in each blank with the correct question word or phrase from the following list.

| How's | How are | What's | What time is |
| Where's | Where are | When's | |

EXAMPLE: Q: __*Where's*__ your school?

A: It's on Main Street.

1. Q: _____ your birthday?
   A: It's in February.

2. Q: _____ the weather?
   A: It's sunny.

3. Q: _____ you from?
   A: I'm from Brazil.

4. Q: _____ your party?
   A: It's at 6:00.

5. Q: _____ your kids?
   A: They're fine.

6. Q: _____ your name?
   A: My name is Helen.

7. Q: _____ my wallet?
   A: It's in the living room.

8. Q: _____ your first language?
   A: My first language is English.

9. Q: _____ Anna and Paul?
   A: They're probably at work.

10. Q: _____ your pancakes?
    A: They're great!

B Circle the correct preposition.

EXAMPLE: The test is (in/on/at) Wednesday. *(on circled)*

1. My party is (in/on/at) 7:00.

2. His birthday is (in/on/at) July 2.

3. My trip is (in/on/at) August.

4. The meeting is (in/on/at) 8:00 in the morning.

5. Her flight is (in/on/at) September 22.

C Read each question. Then check the best answer.

EXAMPLE: When is the test?

_____ It's fun!

___✓___ It's on Wednesday.

_____ No, it's not today.

1. What's his name?

_____ It's windy.

_____ It's Tom.

_____ I'm Tom.

2. How's the weather?

_____ It's sunny.

_____ Yes, it is.

_____ They're sunny.

3. Where are my keys?

_____ There are five keys.

_____ It's probably in the living room.

_____ They're on the table.

4. Where is she from?

_____ English.

_____ American.

_____ New York.

5. What's his nationality?

_____ Mexican.

_____ Mexico.

_____ Spain.

6. What's your first language?

_____ American.

_____ English.

_____ The United States.

7. When is your party?

_____ It's on Saturday.

_____ It's at my house.

_____ It's great!

8. What time is the meeting?

_____ It's on July 21.

_____ It's in August.

_____ It's at 3:00.

9. How's the hamburger?

_____ It's rainy.

_____ It's not very good.

_____ They're fine.

10. How are your sons?

_____ He's busy.

_____ I'm busy.

_____ They're busy.

Review Test: Lessons 22–26

Name _____ Date _____

A Match each question with the correct answer.

1. __j__ How much are those flowers?   a. It's three hours long.

2. _____ Are those shoes expensive?   b. Helen is.

3. _____ How much is that book?   c. It's at 6:00.

4. _____ How old is their son?   d. It's in February.

5. _____ How old are their daughters?   e. Yes, they are.

6. _____ Who else is absent today?   f. They're twelve years old.

7. _____ Is this book interesting?   g. It's about $10.00.

8. _____ When is his birthday?   h. He's fifteen years old.

9. _____ What time is the movie?   i. No, it's not. It's boring.

10. _____ Are there monkeys at the zoo?   j. They're $15.00.

11. _____ How long is the play?   k. Yes, there are.

B Fill in each blank with *in, on, at, from*, or *to*.

EXAMPLE: It's ___in___ January.

1. The movie is _____ 3:00 _____ 5:00.

2. The party is _____ Saturday.

3. The class is _____ 10:00 a.m.

4. My party is _____ Wednesday night.

5. His birthday is _____ September.

C Fill in each blank with *there, their*, or *they're*. Capitalize the word if it is the first word in the sentence.

EXAMPLE: ___They're___ in the living room.

1. Is that _____ son?

2. _____ are two children in the kitchen.

3. _____ my grandparents.

4. _____ grandchildren are in the park.

5. _____ in the house.

D Read each question. Then check the best answer.

EXAMPLE: How much are those books?

_____ There are five books.

_____ They're over there.

___✓___ They're $25.00.

1. How old is your daughter?

_____ She's fifteen years old.

_____ They're fifteen years old.

_____ She's over there.

2. Who's that woman?

_____ Yes, she is.

_____ She's my mother.

_____ She's forty-five years old.

3. How long is the movie?

_____ It's at 3:00.

_____ It's two hours long.

_____ It's on Tuesday.

4. How much is the movie?

_____ It's at 3:00.

_____ It's at the movie theater.

_____ It's $8.00.

5. When's the meeting?

_____ It's at 3:00.

_____ It's three hours long.

_____ Yes, it is.

Review Test: Lessons 27–30

Name _____ Date _____

A Fill in each blank with *s* or *'s*.

EXAMPLE: Those are John _'s_ book _s_ .

1. Helen _____ friend is here.

2. Harry _____ happy today.

3. The chair _____ are in the kitchen.

4. It _____ over there.

5. His son _____ name is Gary.

B Read the first sentence in each item. Then check the true sentence below it.

EXAMPLE: Kathy is Harry's mother.

_____ Harry is Kathy's nephew.

__✓__ Harry is Kathy's son.

_____ Harry is Kathy's husband.

1. Martin is Helen's nephew.

_____Helen is Martin's cousin.

_____ Helen is Martin's aunt.

_____ Helen is Martin's niece.

2. Mark is Mary's grandson.

_____ Mary is Mark's grandmother.

_____ Mary is Mark's mother.

_____ Mary is Mark's aunt.

3. John is Ann's uncle.

_____Ann is John's aunt.

_____Ann is John's cousin.

_____Ann is John's niece.

4. Susan is Charlie's sister.

_____Charlie is Susan's father.

_____Charlie is Susan's nephew.

_____Charlie is Susan's brother.

5. Roberto is Mario's cousin.

_____Mario is Roberto's uncle.

_____Mario is Roberto's cousin.

_____Mario is Roberto's nephew.

C Fill in each blank with *go* or *goes*.

EXAMPLE: Al ____goes____ to the beach on Saturdays.

1. I _____ to school every day.

2. On Wednesdays, Al and Erika _____ to English class.

3. Erika _____ to the library on Sundays.

4. Every summer, we _____ to the mountains.

5. He _____ there at 8:00.

D Fill in each blank with *go, go to,* or *go to the*.

EXAMPLE: We ____go____ there every Sunday.

1. Erika and I _____ work at 7:00.

2. They _____ home at 5:00.

3. Lisa and Ann _____ swimming every day.

4. I _____ park with my friends.

5. You _____ bike-riding in the summer.

Review Test: Lessons 31–34

Name _____ Date _____

A Complete each sentence. Use the correct form of a verb below.

         eat   brush   wake up

                go   take

EXAMPLE: He __*calls*__ his mother twice a month.

1. Sandy _____ a shower every morning.

2. Andy _____ his teeth twice a day.

3. She _____ at 6:00 in the morning.

4. We _____ a good breakfast every day.

5. I _____ to work at 7:30.

B Fill in each blank with the *he/she* form of the verb in parentheses.

EXAMPLE: Helen (go) _____*goes*_____ to the park on Saturdays.

1. Andy (try) _____ to work eight hours a day.

2. Sandy (watch) _____ TV in the morning.

3. Andy (work) _____ at home.

4. Sandy (play) _____ computer games.

5. He (fix) _____ computers.

6. She (stay) _____ at home.

7. Andy (live) _____ in New York.

8. She (miss) _____ her bus sometimes.

9. He (wake up) _____ at 6:00.

10. She (study) _____ English every day.

C Fill in each blank with the correct form of *do, have, make,* or *take.*

EXAMPLE: They ___make___ dinner every day.

1. Sandy and Andy _____ a good time on Saturdays.

2. She _____ her homework every night.

3. They _____ tests every week.

4. Sandy _____ the train to work.

5. He _____ breakfast at 8:00.

D Make each sentence negative using the verb in parentheses.

EXAMPLE: Helen and Tom (do) ___don't do___ the laundry on Saturdays.

1. Sandy and Andy (work) _____ together.

2. He (brush) _____ his teeth every day.

3. She (do) _____ the dishes on Saturday.

4. They (play) _____ computer games every day.

5. We (watch) _____ TV in the morning.

Review Test: Lessons 35–38

Name _____ Date _____

A For each affirmative statement write a yes-no question.

EXAMPLE: They eat breakfast at 8:00.

Do they eat breakfast at 8:00?

1. I have homework.

_____

2. She goes to work at 8:00.

_____

3. They want pizza for dinner.

_____

4. It snows a lot in January.

_____

5. You study hard at night.

_____

6. They always go to bed at 10:00.

_____

7. She teaches English in Chicago.

_____

8. You have to go to the restaurant.

_____

9. He likes my school.

_____

10. John's a student.

_____

B Put the words in the correct order to make statements and questions.

EXAMPLE: on /go/swimming/always/We/Saturday

We always go swimming on Saturday .

1. to/Do/school/you/go/on Mondays

_____?

2. breakfast/7:00/always/at/I/eat

_____ .

3. food/I/some/need/to buy

_____ .

4. do/eat/What/for lunch/you

_____ ?

5. He/never/skiing/December/goes/in

_____ .

6. Do/to/the library/go/they

_____ ?

7. in/Katya/San Francisco/Does/live

_____ ?

8. plays/He/in/rarely/baseball/the winter

_____ .

9. have/every night/I/to study

_____ .

10. you/classes/Why/take/do

_____ ?

C Write a *Wh* question for each answer. Use the question word in parentheses.

EXAMPLE: (what time)__*What time does your class start?*__
My class starts at 7:00.

1. (when) _____
My birthday is in February.

2. (what) _____
He eats cereal for breakfast.

3. (where) _____
She goes to the beach in the summer.

4. (who) _____
I live with my parents.

5. (what time) _____
My class starts at 3:00.

Review Test: Lessons 39–43

Name _____ Date _____

A Fill in each blank with the correct form of the verb in parentheses. Use the present continuous tense.

EXAMPLE: (go) I ____am going____ to school.

1. He (sit) _____ at his desk.

2. They (play) _____ in the park.

3. I (write) _____ a letter.

4. We (swim) _____ in the pool.

5. You (eat) _____ breakfast.

B For each affirmative statement, write a negative statement and a yes-no question.

EXAMPLE: He is playing the piano.

   <u>He isn't playing the piano.</u>
   <u>Is he playing the piano?</u>

1. They're working today.

_____

_____

2. She's doing her homework.

_____

_____

3. You're studying hard.

_____

_____

4. It's raining in New York City.

_____

_____

5. I'm going to the beach.

_____

_____

C Write a *Wh* question for each answer. Use the question word in parentheses.

EXAMPLE: (where)___*Where is Kim going?*_____

Kim is going to the beach.

1. (what) _____
They're eating.

2. (why) _____
He's crying because he's sad.

3. (who) _____
Sue is babysitting.

4. (when) _____
I'm going skiing in December.

5. (where) _____
We're going to Chicago next week.

D Match each question with the correct answer.

1. __d__ Where are you going?   a. John is.

2. _____ How is it going?   b. I'm reading.

3. _____ Who's talking on the phone?   c. After class.

4. _____ Why are you crying?   d. To the movies.

5. _____ When are you going home?   e. Fine.

6. _____ What are you doing?   f. Because I'm sad.

Review Test: Lessons 44–47

Name _____ Date _____

A Fill in each blank with the correct form of the verb in parentheses. Use the present tense or the present continuous tense.

EXAMPLE: Ann (eat)___*is eating*___breakfast now.

1. Peter (get up) _____ at 8:00 every morning.

2. Alex (be) _____ from France.

3. They (come) _____ home at 6:00 today.

4. We (wear) _____ our uniforms every day.

5. He (eat) _____ breakfast right now.

6. I (take) _____ piano lessons twice a week.

7. She (play) _____ tennis on Tuesdays.

8. Right now, I (listen) _____ to some great music!

9. I (go) _____ fishing every weekend.

10. Today, I (work) _____ in my office.

B For each affirmative statement, write a negative statement and a yes-no question.

EXAMPLE: She's going to the movies.

   She isn't going to the movies.

   Is she going to the movies?

1. He can play the piano.

_____

_____

2. She's going to the beach today.

_____

3. They study English on Tuesdays.

_____

_____

4. It rains a lot in the summer.

_____

_____

5. They can speak English.

_____

_____

C Find the mistakes. Rewrite the sentences.

EXAMPLE: She eats breakfast right now.

She is eating breakfast right now. _____

1. He is go skiing every winter.

_____

2. I can to speak English.

_____

3. She can swims.

_____

4. I can speak English, but I can speak Spanish.

_____

5. He wears his uniform now.

_____

Review Test: Lessons 48–51

Name _____ Date _____

A For each affirmative statement, write a negative statement and a yes-no question.

EXAMPLE: She was in Rome last year.

She wasn't in Rome last year.

Was she in Rome last year?

1. He was born in Mexico.

_____

_____

2. John and Ling were home last night.

_____

_____

3. You were at the restaurant yesterday.

_____

_____

4. There was a lot of rain in the summer.

_____

_____

5. It was a good restaurant.

_____

_____

B Match each question with the correct answer.

1. __e__ Were you in Japan last year?   a. It was great!

2. _____ How much was the radio?   b. It was $20.00.

3. _____ Why were you absent?   c. It was three days ago.

4. _____ How was your vacation?   d. January 15, 1949.

5. _____ When was he born?   e. No, I wasn't.

6. _____ Who was on vacation?   f. In New York City.

7. _____ Was she absent two days ago?   g. It was at 3:00.

8. _____ When was his birthday party?   h. It was two hours long.

9. _____ What time was the meeting?   i. Helen was.

10. _____ Where were you born?   j. Yes, she was.

11. _____ How long was the movie?   k. Because I was sick.

C Fill in each blank with *am*, *is*, *are*, *was*, or *were*.

EXAMPLE: Matthew _____was_____ a doctor when he was young.

1. John _____ born in February.

2. My name _____ Ann.

3. The children _____ in the park yesterday.

4. Right now they _____ at home.

5. I _____ a student now.

Review Test: Lessons 52–56

Name _____ Date _____

A Fill in each blank with the past tense form of the verb in parentheses.

EXAMPLE: (drive) They __*drove*__ to Chicago last year.

1. (take) They _____ their friend to the movies.

2. (make) He _____ a delicious salad for lunch.

3. (walk) Helen and Anna _____ to the library this morning.

4. (study) They _____ English all morning.

5. (give) I _____ him ten dollars yesterday.

6. (put) He _____ the salad on the table.

7. (stop) The car _____ near our house.

8. (eat) I _____ dinner about an hour ago.

9. (cry) The baby _____ for an hour.

10. (go) We _____ to San Francisco in August.

B Change each affirmative sentence to a negative sentence.

EXAMPLE: We went to a movie last night.

We didn't go to a movie last night.

1. I cut the vegetables for the salad.

_____

2. Alice married Joe.

_____

3. Andy hugged his son this morning.

_____

4. The teacher smiled at the children.

_____

5. We studied for the test.

_____

C Fill in each blank with *wasn't, weren't,* or *didn't.*

EXAMPLE: They ___*didn't*___ go to school yesterday.

1. He _____ come to the party.

2. John and his friend _____ busy last night.

3. Gretchen _____ in Mexico last summer.

4. I _____ take the bus to work.

5. We _____ students in 1995.

6. It _____ rain yesterday.

7. She _____ eat at a restaurant.

8. It _____ cold in December.

9. Mary and Mika _____ go to school this morning.

10. The test _____ difficult.

Review Test: Lessons 57–60

Name _____ Date _____

A For each affirmative sentence write a yes-no question.

EXAMPLE: He ate dinner at a restaurant last night.
            Did he eat dinner in a restaurant last night?

1. There were a lot of people at the park yesterday.

_____

2. He went skiing in the mountains in December.

_____

3. She slept for a long time.

_____

4. It was sunny on Tuesday.

_____

5. You drove to work yesterday.

_____

B Write a *Wh* question for each answer. Use the question word in parentheses.

EXAMPLE: (what time) The movie started at 8:00.
            What time did the movie start?

1. (who) _____
She went with Juan.

2. (why) _____
He got here late because there was a lot of traffic.

3. where) _____
They ate dinner at a restaurant.

4. (how) _____
She came here by bus.

5. (when) _____
They went to New York last night.

C Match each question with the correct answer.

1. __d__ When did she get home?   a. They went to a movie.

2. _____ What did they do last night?   b. Yes, it was.

3. _____ What time did the movie start?   c. Because I had a big test.

4. _____ How did she get there?   d. Two days ago.

5. _____ Was it a good movie?   e. By plane.

6. _____ Why did you study on Saturday?   f. At 8:00.

D Fill in each blank with a verb in the present continuous, present, or past tense. Use the verb in parentheses.

EXAMPLE: (eat) He___*eats*___ breakfast every day.

1. She (swim) _____ in the pool right now.

2. He (go) _____ to the beach four days last week.

3. They (be) _____ sometimes late for class this semester.

4. I (fly) _____ to China every summer.

5. She (look at) _____ a photo now.

6. She (smile) _____ at me a lot yesterday.

7. He (have) _____ a big problem two weeks ago.

8. The bus (stop) _____ here every day at 6:00 and 10:00.

9. The baby (cry) _____ for an hour last night.

10. My father (be) _____ very happy now.

Review Test: Lessons 61–64

Name _____ Date _____

A Put the following times in the correct order.

the day after tomorrow   next month   in three days

tonight   tomorrow   ~~right now~~

1._____ right now _____

2._____

3._____

4._____

5._____

6._____

B Complete the charts.

Affirmative Statement	You're going to go to Los Angeles.
Negative Statement	
Yes-No Question	Are you going to Los Angeles
Affirmative Statement	
Negative Statement	They're not going to drive to work today.
Yes-No Question	
Affirmative Statement	
Negative Statement	
Yes-No Question	Is she going to clean her room?

C. Write a *Wh* question for each answer. Use the question word in parentheses.

EXAMPLE: (where) We're going to go to Chile.

Where are we going to go?

1. (when) _____
   They are going to study English next year.

2. (how long) _____
   It's going to take two days.

3. (why) _____
   He is going to go to England because he wants to study English.

4. (how) _____
   They are going to go there by bus.

5. (who) _____
   She is going to eat dinner with Mary.

D Put the words in the correct order to make statements and questions.

EXAMPLE: to the movies/They/going/go/to/are

They are going to go to the movies.

1. to school /Are/to/you/going /go

_____?

2. I'm/my friends/visit/to/going

_____.

3. dance/not/He/is/going/to

_____.

4. go/home/time/she/going/What/to/is

_____?

5. to/are/watch/They/TV/going

_____.

Student Book
Answer Key

Introduction: Student Book

A My name is <u>H</u>elen. I am from <u>N</u>ew <u>Y</u>ork.
<u>N</u>ow <u>I</u> live in <u>C</u>alifornia. <u>I</u> am a teacher. <u>I</u> like
teaching and writing books.

B
1. a   b, <u>c</u>, d
2. <u>e</u>   <u>f</u>, g, <u>h</u>
3. <u>i</u>   j, k, l, m, n
4. o   <u>p</u>, q, r, s, t
5. <u>u</u>   v, <u>w</u>, x, <u>y</u>, z

D

1. Vowels:	✓ a	__ z	__ D	✓ u
2. Consonants:	__ I	✓ f	✓ m	__ E
3. Vowels:	__ T	✓ e	__ f	__ N
4. Consonants:	✓ Z	__ o	✓ q	__ A
5. Vowels:	__ F	✓ i	✓ U	__ p
6. Consonants:	__ O	✓ G	✓ c	__ I

Lesson 1: Student Book

A

(a clock) (a grandfather) tables   (a bedroom)   (a mother)
(a kitchen) (a wife)   (a living room) (a husband) sofas
(a lamp) (a backyard)   windows   (a house)   chairs

B

People	Places	Things
a grandfather	a bedroom	a clock
a mother	a kitchen	tables
a wife	a living room	sofas
a husband	a backyard	a lamp
	a house	windows
		chairs

Lesson 2: Student Book

C
1. he 2. I 3. we 4. they 5. you 6. it 7. she 8. he 9. it 10. you

Lesson 3: Student Book

A
1. b 2. c 3. a 4. d

B
1. a 2. d 3. b 4. c

Lesson 4: Student Book

A
1. kitchen
2. expensive
3. desk
4. classroom
5. happy

Review Lessons 1–4: Student Book

A
1.

People a father, a boy, a mother, a baby,

Things Possible answers: a chair, a bottle, a sink, dish(es), a table, a dog, a basket, clothes, a clock, a cup, a teabag, a window, a radio/radios, a box
2. & 3. Various answers are possible.
4. Circled verbs: hold, listen, wash, sleep, sit, stand, cry, smile, drink

Have Fun Lessons1–4: Student Book

A
1. student 2. teacher 3. study 4. happy 5. run 6. cheap 7. big 8. table 9. walk

B

Nouns	Verbs	Adjectives
student	*study*	*happy*
teacher	*run*	*cheap*
table	*walk*	*big*

Lesson 5: Student Book

A
1. Juan is a college student. He's very busy. He's at school every day.
2. Paul and I are twins. We're 16 years old. We're high school students. I'm a basketball player. My brother is a soccer player.
3. Patricia is a waitress in a big restaurant. She's tired. Peter is a waiter. He's happy.
4. Phuong is an architect. She's the boss in her office. Her office is beautiful. It's in a tall building.

B

Hi! My name ____*is*____ George. I ____*am*____ an English teacher. I ____*am*____ from the United States. Gabriela ____*is*____ my wife. She ____*is*____ an English teacher, too. We ____*are*____ happy together.

Hello! My name ____*is*____ Gabriela. George ____*is*____ my husband. We ____*are*____ married and we ____*are*____ teachers. We ____*are*____ from different countries. I ____*am*____ from Argentina, and George ____*is*____ from the United States.

C

People say:	You say:
1. I'm_ a doctor.	He's a doctor.
2. We're_ students.	They're students.
3. I'm_ an architect.	She's an architect.
4. I'm_ a waiter.	He's a waiter.
5. I'm_ a waitress.	She's a waitress.
6. I'm_ a teacher.	You're_ a teacher.

Lesson 6: Student Book

A

1. (b) They aren't happy.
2. (c) You're not old.
3. (c) He's not tall.
4. (b) It isn't cold.
5. (a) It's blue.
6. (c) She isn't sad.
7. (b) We're not short.
8. (c) I'm young.

B

1. It's not bad!/It isn't bad!
2. You're not late!/You aren't late!
3. It's not beautiful!/It isn't beautiful!
4. I'm not tall!

C

1. We aren't single./We're not single.
2. They aren't single./They're not single.
3. We aren't old./We're not old.
4. She isn't late./She's not late.
5. They aren't short./They're not short.
6. You aren't slow./You're not slow.

Lesson 7: Student Book

A

1. It's an expensive jewelry store.
2. It's a crowded bookstore.
3. It's a noisy music store.
4. They're friendly salespeople.
5. They're happy children.
6. It's a great restaurant.
7. She's a young waitress.
8. He's an old waiter.

B

1. The jewelry store isn't expensive.	It isn't an expensive jewelry store.
2. The bookstore isn't crowded.	It isn't a crowded bookstore.
3. The music store isn't noisy.	It isn't a noisy music store.
4. The salespeople aren't friendly.	They aren't friendly salespeople.
5. The children aren't happy.	They aren't happy children.
6. The restaurant isn't great.	It isn't a great restaurant.
7. The waitress isn't young.	She isn't a young waitress.
8. The waiter isn't old.	He isn't an old waiter.

Lesson 8: Student Book

A

1. Susan is always early for work.
2. Sometimes Steve is late for work./Steve is sometimes late for work./Steve is late for work sometimes.
3. Sometimes Susan and Steve are absent from school./Susan and Steve are sometimes absent from school./Susan and Steve are absent from school sometimes.
4. Mr. and Mrs. Clay are often busy.
5. Mrs. Clay is never late.
6. The family is often at home.
7. The children are usually busy with school and work.
8. Steve is always at school on Mondays.
9. They are usually late for school.
10. Susan is never home on Saturdays.
11. Steve is always on time for dinner.

B

1 a. T b. F c. F
2 a. F b. T c. T
3 a. T b. F c. F

C Answers may vary.

Review Lessons 5–8: Student Book

A

A: Are you a student?
B: Yes, I am.
A: Are you always busy?
B: Yes, I am!

B

1. Ellen is a busy person.
2. Ellen is a student.
3. Ellen is always a good student.
4. She is also a waitress.
5. The restaurant is great.
6. It is an expensive restaurant.
7. It isn't cheap.
8. The waiters and waitresses are busy.
9. The restaurant is usually crowded.
10. The food is good.
11. People are happy in the restaurant.
12. People aren't quiet in the restaurant.
13. She is often tired in the morning.
14. She is never early for work.
15. Susan isn't early for work.
16. Her apartment is beautiful.
17. Her friends are often in her apartment./Her friend is often in her apartment.
18. They are nice people.
19. Sometimes they are noisy.
20. Ellen is a happy person.

C

Danny

Danny is six years old. He's a happy child. He's a student in a big school. He is a good student. He isn't noisy. He isn't bad. He's never late for school. He is always on time. Sometimes he is early.

Danny and Melissa

Danny and Melissa are six years old. They are/They're happy children. They are/They're students in a big school. They are good students. They're not/They aren't noisy. They're not/They aren't bad. They're never late for school. They are always on time. Sometimes they are early.

Have Fun Lessons 5–8: Student Book

Word Search

```
C  K  L  P  M  N  L  H  S
H  U  Y  D  E  M  A  O  E
F  R  I  V  Q  E  L  F  M
A  S  E  L  A  P  W  T  I
P  R  N  X  C  V  A  E  T
U  S  U  A  L  L  Y  N  E
J  T  I  B  Z  R  S  O  M
Y  B  D  N  N  E  T  F  O
N  I  A  C  R  T  Y  E  S
```

Lesson 9: Student Book

A

But there's a nice living room and a big kitchen.
And there are two small bedrooms.
There's a dining room, too.
And there's a yard.

B

1. There is a living room.
2. There is a sofa in the living room.
3. There is a coffee table in front of the sofa.
4. There are end tables next to the sofa.
5. There are pictures on the wall.
6. There is a big kitchen.
7. There is a table in the kitchen.
8. There are six chairs around the table.
9. There is a refrigerator in the corner of the kitchen.
10. There are two pots and a pan on the stove.
11. There is one bed in the bedroom.
12. There are pillows on the bed.
13. There are night tables next to the bed.
14. There is a dresser near the door.
15. There is a TV on the dresser.
16. There is a barbeque in the yard.
17. There is a table in the yard.
18. There are chairs around the table.
19. There are flowers in the yard.
20. There is a dog in the yard.

A
1. Yes, I am.
2. Yes, I am.
3. No, I'm not.
4. No, I'm not.
5. Yes, I am.
6. No, I'm not.
7. No, I'm not.
8. Yes, I am.
9. Yes, I am.
10. Yes, she is.
11. Yes, I am.

B
1. Are they in a park?   Yes, they are.
2. Are they happy?   Yes, they are.
3. Is it sunny?   Yes, it is.
4. Is it cloudy?   No, it isn't.
5. Is he at work?   Yes, he is.
6. Is he at home?   No, he isn't.

C
1. They're in a park.
2. They're happy.
3. It's sunny.
4. He's at work.
5. He's a man.

Lesson 11: Student Book

A
Are there schools near here?   Yes, there are.
Are there many kids in this building?   Yes, there are a lot of kids.
And is there a supermarket nearby?   Yes, there is.
Is there a mall?   No, there isn't.

B
1. Yes, there is.
2. Yes, there is.
3. Yes, there are.
4. Yes, there are.
5. No, there isn't.
6. Yes, there are.

C
1. Is there a playground nearby?   Yes, there is.
2. Are there people in the parking lot?   No, there aren't.
3. Are there shops in the neighborhood?   Yes, there are.
4. Is there a movie theater around the corner from the shoe store?   Yes, there is.
5. Is there a school next to the supermarket?   No, there isn't.
6. Are there cars in the parking lot?   Yes, there are.

D

1. <u>Is</u> there a yard?
2. <u>Is</u> there a playground?
3. <u>Is</u> there a movie theatre in your neighborhood?
4. <u>Is</u> there a supermarket in your neighborhood?
5. <u>Are</u> there schools in your neighborhood?
6. <u>Are</u> there shops nearby?

Review Lessons 9–11: Student Book

A

My house is old, but it's nice. There's a big living room and a big kitchen. There are two small bedrooms and one bathroom. There's a small yard with a big tree.

C

1. <u>Are</u> you a student?
2. <u>Are</u> you married?
3. <u>Are</u> you at home?
4. <u>Is</u> it sunny today?
5. <u>Is</u> the teacher in the classroom?
6. <u>Is</u> the door open?
7. <u>Are</u> the windows closed?
8. <u>Are</u> the windows open?
9. <u>Are</u> there a lot of students in the class?
10. <u>Are</u> the students friendly?
11. <u>Is</u> this exercise easy?
12. <u>Is</u> this exercise difficult?

D

1. Is there a clock in your classroom?
2. Is there a computer in your classroom?
3. Are there students in your classroom?
4. Are there desks in your classroom?
5. Are there windows in your classroom?

E

1. English is easy.
2. Is English easy?
3. The students are friendly.
4. Are the students friendly?
5. I am never late for class.
6. We are usually home at 6:00 p.m.
7. Susan is never absent.
8. They are always on time.

Have Fun Lessons 9–11: Student Book

A

Questions

1. Is there a TV in the living room?
2. Is there a couch?
3. Is there a lamp?
4. Are there pictures?
5. Is there a table?
6. Are there chairs?

7. Is there a computer?
8. Are there people?
9. Is there a dog?
10. Is there a bird?

Answers for Student A
1. Yes, there is.
2. Yes, there is.
3. Yes, there is.
4. Yes, there are.
5. Yes, there is.
6. No, there aren't.
7. No, there isn't.
8. No, there aren't.
9. Yes, there is.
10. No, there isn't.

Answers for Student B
1. Yes, there is.
2. Yes, there is.
3. No, there isn't.
4. No, there aren't.
5. Yes, there is.
6. Yes, there are.
7. Yes, there is.
8. Yes, there are.
9. No, there isn't.
10. Yes, there is.

Lesson 12: Student Book

A

<u>This is</u> a great city, Anna.
<u>This is</u> the library.
<u>That's</u> City Hall.
And <u>that's</u> a famous park.
No. <u>That's</u> a person.
Well, <u>this is</u> a good restaurant.

B

1. Is the library *close to* or *far from* the women?	(close to)	far from
2. Is City Hall *close to* or *far from* the women?	close to	(far from)
3. Is the park *close to* or *far from* the women?	close to	(far from)
4. Are the street entertainers *close to* or *far from* the women?	close to	(far from)

C

1. <u>This is</u> a nice museum.
2. <u>That's</u> a famous clock.
3. <u>That's</u> a famous bridge.
4. <u>This is</u> a good restaurant.

Lesson 13: Student Book

A

Hi, I'm Ricky. This is my room. This is my bed. That's my closet. (These are/ (Those are)) my clothes. And ((these are)/those are) my shoes (These are)/Those are) my fish. I have three fish. ((These are)/Those are) my books. (These are/(Those are)) my toys next to the closet. My mom wants me to clean my room.

B

	Close to Ricky	Far from Ricky
1. <u>Those are</u> my clothes.		✓
2. <u>Those are</u> my shoes.		✓
3. <u>These are</u> my fish.	✓	
4. <u>Those are</u> my toys.		✓
5. <u>These are</u> my books.	✓	

C

1. <u>These are</u> my grandparents.
2. <u>Those are</u> my parents.
3. <u>Those are</u> my sisters.
4. <u>These are</u> my brothers.

Lesson 14: Student Book

A

1. (This is) my living room.
2. (That's) my stereo.
3. (Those are) my CDs.
4. And (this is) my TV.
5. (This is) my favorite room.
6. (These are) my new chairs.
7. (This is) my bedroom.
8. (That's) my brother's bedroom.
9. (Those are) my three cars.
10. And (this is) my garden.

B

Andrew says:	Close To	Far From	Singular	Plural
1. *These are* my watches.	✓			✓
2. *That's* my swimming pool.		✓	✓	
3. *This is* my boat.	✓		✓	
4. *Those are* my computers.		✓		✓
5. *That's* my big TV.		✓	✓	
6. *These are* my DVDs.	✓			✓
7. *This is* my garden.	✓		✓	
8. *Those are* my motorcycles.		✓		✓

Lesson 15: Student Book

A

<u>Will, is this your CD?</u>
<u>Is that your clock under the bed?</u>
<u>Hey, Bill—are these your keys?</u>
<u>Are those your socks, Phil?</u>

B

1. Is this your CD?
2. Are these my socks?
3. Is that his shirt?
4. Are those my shoes?
5. Is this my watch?
6. Is that her TV?
7. Are these your keys?
8. Are those her keys?

C

Bill: ~~This is~~ ^{Is this} your shirt, Phil?

Phil: Yes, it is. ~~These are~~ ^{Are these} your socks?

Bill: No, they aren't.

Phil: Will, ~~these are~~ ^{are these} your socks?

Will: Yes, they are. And those are my jeans.

Phil: No, they're *my* jeans!

Will: Oh, you're right. ~~That is~~ ^{Is that} my shirt?

Bill: Yes, it is. ~~These are~~ ^{Are these} your shorts?

Phil: No, they aren't. Those are *my* shorts.

Lesson 16: Student Book

A

What's <u>this</u>?
OK. And what's <u>that</u>?
What are <u>those</u>?
And what are <u>these</u>?

B

1. Q: What's this?
   A: It's a telephone.
2. Q: What are those?
   A: They're telephones.
3. Q: What are those?
   A: They're stereos.
4. Q: What's this?
   A: It's a stereo.
5. Q: What are these?
   A: They're TVs.
6. Q: What's that?
   A: It's a TV.
7. Q: What's that?
   A: It's a telephone.
8. Q: What are these?
   A: They're stereos.

Review Lessons 12–16: Student Book

A

A: Is this your pen?
B: Yes, it is. Thanks.
A: And are these your keys?
B: No, they're not my keys.

B

(This is/<u>These are</u>) my parents.
And (<u>this is</u>/these are) my older brother.
 (Is this/<u>Are these</u>) your children?
No, (it's/<u>they're</u>) not.
They're (your/<u>my</u>) grandchildren.
What is (<u>that</u>/those)?
Oh, (<u>that's</u>/those are) a famous art museum.
(Is this/<u>Are these</u>) your friends?
Yes, (it is/<u>they are</u>).
(This is/<u>These are</u>) wonderful photos.

C

Singular	Plural
1. This is my DVD.	These are my DVDs.
2. That is my classmate.	Those are my classmates.
3. Is this your book?	Are these your books?
4. Is that your car?	Are those your cars?
5. What's this?	What are these?
6. What is that?	What are those?

D

1. Are those your roommates? Yes, they are.
2. Is this your test? Yes, it is.
3. Is that your car? Yes, it is.
4. Are these your socks? Yes, they are.
5. Is this your coat? Yes, it is.
6. Is that the Eiffel Tower? Yes, it is.

Have Fun Lessons 12–16: Student Book

A Word Search

This is my _____ apartment.   This is my _____ house.

This is my _____ bed.   These are my _____ keys.

This is my _____ bedroom.   These are my _____ neighbors.

These are my _____ brothers.   These are my _____ parents.

These are my _____ clothes.   This is my _____ school.

This is my _____ desk.   These are my _____ shoes.

This is my _____ garden.   These are my _____ socks.

G	B	A	D	Y	D	C	T	L	S
A	R	M	G	E	L	F	N	S	T
R	O	L	S	O	B	E	E	J	N
D	T	K	T	J	E	S	M	V	E
E	H	H	F	A	T	U	T	P	R
N	E	I	G	H	B	O	R	S	A
S	R	S	Y	E	K	H	A	O	P
M	S	C	H	O	O	L	P	C	N
S	E	O	H	S	R	A	A	K	C
M	O	O	R	D	E	B	I	S	L

Lesson 17: Student Book

A

What's her name?
What's her last name?
What's his name?
And I think his last name is Newman.

B
1. <u>What's</u> her last name? Her last name is Rivera.
2. <u>What's</u> her middle name? Her middle name is Rosa.
3. <u>What's</u> her address? Her address is 2630 Beach Avenue,
  Beverly Hills, CA 90210.
4. <u>What's</u> her date of birth? Her date of birth is July 5, 1972.
5. <u>What's</u> her license number? Her license number is N9234857.

C
1. <u>What's</u> your first name?
2. <u>What's</u> your last name?
3. <u>What's</u> your address?
4. <u>What's</u> your phone number?

Lesson 18: Student Book

A
1. Where <u>is</u> my pen?
2. Where <u>are</u> my glasses?
3. Where <u>are</u> my keys?
4. And where <u>is</u> my car?
5. Where <u>is</u> Katie?
6. Where <u>is</u> your father?

B
1. Where are my books? They're on the floor.
2. Where are the potatoes? They're on the counter.
3. Where's Charlie? He's in the kitchen.
4. Where's Molly? She's at work.
5. Where are Katie and Andy? They're at school.
6. Where's Tuck? He's on the floor./He's at home.

Lesson 19: Student Book

A

Hi! My name is Melissa. I live in a very international neighborhood. It's great! I'm <u>American</u>—I'm from the <u>U.S.</u> and I speak <u>English</u>.

My next-door neighbors, Rika and Hiroshi, are from <u>Japan</u>. They speak <u>Japanese</u>. They often make delicious Japanese food for me. My other next-door neighbors, Ana and Daniel, are from <u>Mexico</u>. They speak <u>Spanish</u>. I like my neighbors a lot.

There are many international restaurants in our neighborhood. There are two <u>Mexican</u> restaurants, three <u>Chinese</u> restaurants, an <u>Indian</u> restaurant, and an Iranian restaurant. People from <u>Mexico</u> work in the <u>Mexican</u> restaurants. People from <u>China</u> work in the <u>Chinese</u> restaurants. People from <u>India</u> work in the <u>Indian</u> restaurant. And people from <u>Iran</u> work in the <u>Iranian</u> restaurant.

I love my international neighborhood.

B
1. (Melissa) <u>Where is she from</u>? She's from <u>the U.S.</u>
2. (Melissa) <u>What's her first language?</u> Her first language is <u>English</u>.
3. (Rika) <u>What's her</u> nationality? She's <u>Japanese</u>.
4. (Rika) <u>Where is she from?</u> She's from <u>Japan</u>.
5. (Ana and Daniel) <u>What's their</u> nationality? They are <u>Mexican</u>.
6. (Ana and Daniel) <u>What's their</u> first language? Their first language is <u>Spanish</u>.

Lesson 20: Student Book

A

<u>What time</u> is your flight to New York?
<u>When</u> is your meeting with Mr. Kim, Ellen?
<u>When</u> is your trip to New York?
Hey <u>what time</u> is our meeting today?
<u>What time</u> is it?

B

1. <u>at</u>
2. in
3. on
4. on
5. at
6. on, at

C

1. <u>When is her meeting?</u>   <u>Her</u> meeting is <u>on</u> Tuesday.
2. <u>When is her trip?</u>   <u>Her</u> trip is <u>in</u> July.
3. <u>When is their flight?</u>   <u>Their</u> flight is <u>at</u> 11 p.m.
4. <u>What time is their meeting?</u>   It's <u>at</u> 2:00.

Lesson 21: Student Book

A

<u>How is</u> the beach?
<u>How is</u> the weather?
<u>How are</u> your kids?
<u>How are</u> you?
<u>How is</u> work?

B

1. <u>How is</u> your hamburger? <u>It's</u> delicious.
2. <u>How are</u> your eggs? <u>They're</u> not bad.
3. <u>How are</u> your fries? <u>They're</u> very good.
4. <u>How is</u> your soup? <u>It's</u> spicy.
5. <u>How are</u> your vegetables? <u>They're</u> terrible!
6. <u>How are</u> your pancakes? <u>They're</u> cold.
7. <u>How is</u> your sandwich? <u>It's</u> great.
8. <u>How is</u> your salad? <u>It's</u> OK.

Review Lessons 17-21: Student Book

A

A: What's that?
B: It's a present for my mother.
A: When is her birthday?
B: It's today.

B

1. What's his name?
2. What's his address?
3. Where is he from?
4. What's his first language?
5. What's his nationality?
6. When is his birthday?
7. When is his class?
8. What time is his class?
9. How is his writing class?
10. How are his classes?

C

Prepositions of Time

in	June	in	July	at	8 a.m.
on	Thursday	on	January 1st	on	July 21st
at	midnight	on	Tuesday	at	9 p.m.

Prepositions of Location

in	the living room	in	the kitchen	at	school
at/on	the table	on	the floor	in	the bathroom
in	my pocket	at	home	at	work

D

1. Hi. <u>My</u> name is Olivia. Here are some photos of <u>my</u> family.
2. This is <u>my</u> brother and this is <u>his</u> wife. They live in New York with <u>their</u> two children.
3. This is <u>my</u> sister and <u>her</u> new boyfriend.
4. These are <u>my</u> parents. They live in Peru, but all <u>their</u> children live in the U.S.

Have Fun Lessons 17–21: Student Book

A

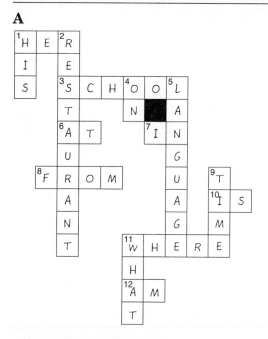

Lesson 22: Student Book

A

<u>This store</u> is really crowded today.
Look—<u>these shoes</u> are nice.
Maybe <u>those shoes</u> over there aren't expensive.
How much are <u>these shoes</u>?

B

	Near	Far	Singular	Plural
1. These jeans are great.	✓			✓
2. That T-shirt is cheap.		✓	✓	
3. These clothes are expensive.	✓			✓
4. This store is crowded.	✓		✓	
5. Those customers aren't friendly		✓		✓
6. These glasses are nice.	✓			✓

C

1. <u>These jackets are expensive.</u>
2. <u>Those watches aren't big.</u>
3. <u>Those belts are brown.</u>
4. <u>This dress is beautiful.</u>
5. <u>That suit isn't your size.</u>
6. <u>This coat isn't warm.</u>

Lesson 23: Student Book

A

How much <u>is</u> this lamp?
How much <u>are</u> those two big lamps over there?
How old <u>are</u> they?
How old <u>are</u> you?
And how old <u>is</u> your little brother?

B

1. It's $12.50.
2. They're $15.00 each.
3. They're $23.00.
4. They're about ten years old.
5. She's five years old.
6. He's one year old.

C

1. How much is the radio?
2. How much is the (antique) typewriter?
3. How old is the typewriter?
4. How old are the telephones?
5. How much are the telephones?
6. How much is the set of dishes?/How much are the dishes?
7. How much is the big vase?
8. How much is the small vase?

Lesson 24

A

<u>a</u>	1.
<u>c</u>	2.
<u>b</u>	3.
<u>f/g</u>	4.
<u>f/g</u>	5.
<u>a</u>	6.
<u>d</u>	7.
<u>g</u>	8.
<u>e</u>	9.

B

1. <u>Who's a doctor?</u>
2. <u>Who's from China?</u>
3. <u>Who's from</u> Mexico?
4. <u>Who else is from</u> Mexico?

Lesson 25: Student Book

A

<u>When is it?</u>
<u>What time?</u>
<u>How long is the movie?</u>

B

It's <u>on</u> Saturday.
It's <u>at</u> 7:00.
It's <u>from</u> 7:00 <u>to</u> 9:00.
It's <u>on</u> Friday mornings.
It's <u>from</u> 8:00 <u>to</u> 8:45.
I get up <u>at</u> 9:00 every day!
I think there's also a class <u>at</u> 10:00 or 11:00.

Lesson 26: Student Book

A

Grandma and Grandpa are at the zoo with <u>their</u> two grandchildren, Diana and Larry. <u>They're</u> all very happy. <u>There</u> is a big section with monkeys. When they go <u>there</u>, Diana says, "Look over <u>there</u>! <u>There</u> are three baby monkeys! <u>Their</u> mother is under the tree with them." Larry says, "And <u>their</u> father is <u>there</u> too. He's in the tree. <u>They're</u> all together."

There (place)	**There is/There are**	**Their**	**They're**
3	2	3	2

B

1. *Their* grandmother is 70 years old.
2. <u>There</u> are two children in <u>their</u> family.
3. <u>They're</u> young.
4. <u>There</u> is a monkey in the tree.
5. <u>They're</u> at the zoo.
6. <u>There</u> is a gorilla over <u>there</u>.
7. <u>There</u> is one gorilla over here, and <u>there</u> are two gorillas over <u>there</u>.
8. <u>They're</u> big gorillas.
9. The children and <u>their</u> grandfather are happy today.

C

1. Their car is hot. It's in the sun.
2. They're thirsty. They want water.
3. Correct
4. Their grandparents are at the zoo.
5. They're at the gift shop.
6. Correct
7. Their parents aren't there.
8. Correct
9. It's time for lunch. They're hungry.
10. Correct

D

1. Their day at the zoo is fun.
2. It's sunny there.
3. At the end of the day, they're tired, but they're happy.

Review Lessons 22–26: Student Book

A
A: These shoes are beautiful.
B: But they're very expensive.
A: Look over there. Those shoes are on sale.
B: How much are they?
A: They're only $30.

B
1. It's on Monday at 12:00 noon.
2. It's from 2:00 to 4:00 p.m./It's two hours long./Two hours.
3. It's at 8:00 a.m. (on Tuesday, November 5).
4. It's on Tuesday, November 5.
5. It's on Tuesday, November 5.
6. It's from 4:00 to 6:00 p.m./It's two hours long./Two hours.
7. It's at 10:00 a.m. (on Monday, November 4).
8. It's on Tuesday (, November 5).
9. It's at 9:00 a.m (on Tuesday, November 5).

C
1. How long is the listening course?
2. How long is the grammar course?
3. What time is the grammar course?
4. How much is the grammar course?
5. When is the grammar course?
6. How much is the listening course?
7. How much are the listening and grammar courses?
8. What time/How long is the grammar course?
9. What time/How long is the listening course?
10. How long are the grammar and listening courses?
11. How old is the school?

D
     I have two children, a boy and a girl. <u>Their</u> names are David and Susan. <u>They're</u> very cute. David is eight years old and Susan is six years old. <u>They're</u> both students. <u>Their</u> school is near our house. <u>There</u> are many students at <u>their</u> school.

Have Fun Lessons 22–26: Student Book

B
1. These
2. Those
3. How long
4. That
5. How much
6. When
7. What time
8. Who

A

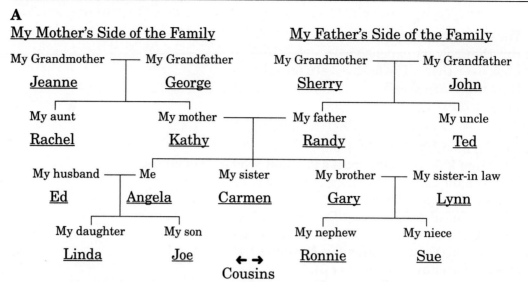

My Mother's Side of the Family   My Father's Side of the Family

My Grandmother ⎯⎯ My Grandfather   My Grandmother ⎯⎯ My Grandfather

Jeanne   George   Sherry   John

My aunt   My mother ⎯⎯ My father   My uncle

Rachel   Kathy   Randy   Ted

My husband ⎯⎯ Me   My sister   My brother ⎯⎯ My sister-in law

Ed   Angela   Carmen   Gary   Lynn

My daughter   My son   My nephew   My niece

Linda   Joe   ← →   Ronnie   Sue

Cousins

B

1. My <u>grandmother's</u> name is Jeanne.
2. Kathy is my <u>mother's</u> name.
3. My <u>husband's</u> name is Ed. I love him very much.
4. My <u>sister's</u> name is Carmen and my <u>brother's</u> name is Gary.
5. My <u>son's</u> name is Joe and my <u>daughter's</u> name is Linda.
6. Angela is <u>Ed's</u> wife.
7. Joe is <u>Ronnie's/Sue's</u> cousin.
8. Joe is <u>Linda's</u> brother.
9. Sue is <u>Angela's/Ed's/Carmen's</u> niece.
10. Ronnie is <u>Angela's/Ed's/Carmen's</u> nephew.

C

1. My daughter's desk is messy.
2. My husband's car is clean.
3. Our dog's bed is dirty.
4. Our neighbor's dog is friendly.
5. Linda's room is big.
6. My son's room is big, too.
7. My daughter's books are on her bed.
8. Carmen's apartment is near my house.

Lesson 28: Student Book

A

1. contracted *S*
2. contracted *S*
3. contracted *S*
4. contracted *S*
5. plural *S*
6. possessive *S*
7. plural *S*
8. possessive *S*
9. plural *S*
10. plural *S*

B

Today is Kevin'<u>s</u> birthday. His friend<u>s</u> are at his apartment. His parent<u>s</u> aren't there. Kevin'<u>s</u> parent<u>s</u> sent twenty-one dollar<u>s</u> to Kevin. He'<u>s</u> very happy. And his sister<u>s</u> sent him two CD<u>s</u>. Kevin'<u>s</u> in his living room with his friend<u>s</u>. They like the new CDs.

C

1. Kevin'<u>s</u> under the kitchen table.
2. Kevin'<u>s</u> two new book<u>s</u> are in the refrigerator.
3. His birthday card<u>s</u> are upside down.
4. The CD<u>s</u> are on the wall. They aren't in the CD player
5. Kevin'<u>s</u> flower<u>s</u> are in a pot on the stove. They aren't in a vase.

Lesson 29: Student Book

A

<u>i</u> 1.
<u>b</u> 2.
<u>f</u> 3.
<u>e</u> 4.
<u>a</u> 5.
<u>c</u> 6.
<u>h</u> 7.
<u>g</u> 8.
<u>d</u> 9.

B

1. goes
2. goes
3. go
4. go
5. go
6. go
7. go
8. go
9. goes
10. goes

C

1. go to the
2. go to
3. go to the
4. go
5. go to the
6. go to

D

1. goes to
2. goes
3. goes to
4. goes to
5. goes to the
6. goes to the

Lesson 30: Student Book

A

1. summer   2. summer   3. fall
4. winter   5. spring   6. winter

B

1. goes bike-riding
2. go ice-skating
3. goes bowling
4. goes swimming
5. goes ice-skating
6. go bike-riding

Review Lessons 27–30: Student Book

A

1. Every day my daughter goes to school at 8:00 a.m.
2. My husband goes to work at 6:00 a.m.
3. We go bike riding every Saturday.
4. I go to the store on Wednesdays.

C

GO	GO TO	GO TO THE
downtown	school	doctor
home	work	mall
outside	bed	library
swimming	Mexico	mountains
sightseeing	Tim's house	beach

D

1. My mother's name is Susan.
2. My brother goes to school every day.
3. This is my teacher's book.
4. The children go to bed early.
5. I go home at 5:00 p.m.
6. I have three children, two boys and a girl.
7. I go shopping.
8. I go to work./I'm going to work.
9. My teacher's name is Charlie.

E

    Kelly is very busy on weekends. Every Saturday morning, she goes to the gym. After that, she goes shopping. She goes to the supermarket and the farmer's market. Sometimes on Saturday afternoons, she goes to her friend's house. On Saturday evenings, she goes to the movies, or she goes dancing with her friends.

Have Fun Lessons 27–30: Student Book

A

1. go to the beach
2. go to bed
3. go dancing
4. go there
5. go to the doctor
6. go downtown
7. go home
8. go to the library
9. go to work
10. go to the movies
11. go to school
12. go upstairs
10. go to the movies
13. go shopping
14. go swimming

Lesson 31: Student Book

A

A. 1, B. 6, C. 5, D. 3, E. 2, F. 4

B

1. wake up, wakes up, 2. get up, gets up, 3. brush, brushes, 4. take, takes, 5. eat, eats, 6. go, goes

Lesson 32: Student Book

A

Sandy <u>lives</u> in New York with her husband Andy. Every morning, Sandy <u>gets up</u> early and <u>goes</u> to work. She <u>works</u> in the city at a software company. She <u>takes</u> her laptop computer to work every day. Sometimes she <u>plays</u> computer games on the train when she <u>goes</u> to work.

Andy <u>works</u> at home. He <u>writes</u> computer programs. He <u>gets up</u> around 9:00 a.m. After he <u>brushes</u> his teeth, he <u>makes</u> breakfast and <u>watches</u> TV. He <u>tries</u> to work eight hours a day, but sometimes he <u>works</u> six or ten hours. When he <u>takes</u> a break, he <u>plays</u> the guitar.

Verbs	Rule Numbers	Verbs	Rule Numbers	Verbs	Rule Numbers
lives	1	takes	1	makes	1
gets up	1	plays	1	watches	2
goes	4	writes	1	tries	3
works	1	brushes	2		

B

1. wakes up
2. gets up
3. gets out of bed
4. brushes her teeth
5. washes her face
6. takes a shower
7. washes her hair
8. gets dressed
9. eats breakfast
10. coffee
11. goes to work
12. takes the train
13. misses the bus
14. stays home
15. walks the dog
16. makes dinner
17. studies English
18. fixes computers

Lesson 33: Student Book

A

A. 7, B. 5, C. 3, D. 4, E. 2, F. 1, G. 6

B

1. has
2. has/makes
3. have/make
4. makes
5. takes
6. does
7. take
8. does
9. makes
10. takes
11. take
12. takes

Lesson 34: Student Book

A

1. _A_ Sandy <u>gets up</u> at 6:15
    _N_ Andy <u>doesn't get up</u> at 6:15.
2. _A_ Sandy <u>goes</u> to work in the city.
    _N_ Andy <u>doesn't work</u> in the city.
3. _A_ Sandy <u>plays</u> computer games.
    _A_ Andy <u>plays</u> the guitar.
4. _N_ Sandy <u>doesn't make</u> dinner.
    _A_ Andy <u>makes</u> dinner.
5. _N_ They <u>don't go</u> to restaurants a lot.
    _A_ Andy <u>is</u> a good cook.

6. __N__ They <u>don't go</u> to the movies a lot.
   __A__ They <u>read</u> newspapers and magazines and watch TV.
7. __N__ They <u>don't go</u> to bed very late.
   __A__ They <u>go</u> to bed around 10:00.

B
1. He doesn't work in the city.
2. He doesn't write books.
3. He doesn't get up at 7:00 a.m.
4. He doesn't take a break in the morning.
5. He doesn't play the piano.
6. He doesn't do the laundry on Thursdays.

C
1. They don't use typewriters.
2. They don't work with typewriters.
3. They don't have dinner at 9:00.
4. They don't watch TV in the afternoon.
5. They don't talk during lunch.
6. They don't take a walk after lunch.

D
1. I <u>don't have</u> breakfast at 10:00 a.m.
2. You <u>don't have</u> lunch at 3:00 p.m.
3. He <u>doesn't have</u> dinner at 9:00 p.m.
4. We <u>don't have</u> a snack at 11:00 p.m.
5. They <u>don't have</u> a good time at work.
6. She <u>doesn't do</u> laundry once a week.
7. He <u>doesn't do</u> laundry twice a week.
8. They <u>don't do</u> laundry three times a week.
9. I <u>don't do</u> my homework in the afternoon.
10. You <u>don't make</u> your bed.
11. We <u>don't make</u> mistakes a lot.
12. She <u>doesn't make</u> a lot of mistakes.
13. They <u>don't take</u> tests every week.
14. I <u>don't take</u> the bus to school.
15. You <u>don't take</u> a break in the morning.
16. He <u>doesn't take</u> a nap every day.
17. It <u>doesn't rain</u> in the summer.
18. It <u>doesn't sleep</u> in the house.

Review Lessons 31–34: Student Book

A
1. Sometimes I'm lazy.
2. I get up late.
3. I don't make my bed.
4. I don't do my laundry.
5. My mother doesn't like that.

B

-s	-es	-ies
gets	brushes	carries
plays	goes	tries
wakes	does	studies
takes	washes	
stays	fixes	
walks	misses	
makes	watches	
works		

C

1. Every morning, my brother <u>washes</u> his face, <u>brushes</u> his teeth, and <u>gets</u> dressed.
2. He <u>takes</u> the bus to school. Sometimes he <u>gets</u> up late, and <u>misses</u> the bus.
3. He <u>works</u> hard at school. After school, he <u>plays</u> soccor.
4. Whe he <u>gets</u> home, he <u>walks</u> the dog and <u>plays</u> the guitar.
5. After dinner, he <u>does</u> his homework.
6. He <u>takes</u> a shower at 9:00 p.m. And he <u>goes</u> to bed at 10:00 p.m.

D

1. Affirmative: He plays soccer. / They play soccer.
   Negative: He doesn't play soccer. / They don't play soccer.
2. Affirmative: She goes to school. / We go to school.
   Negative: She doesn't go to school. / We don't go to school.
3. Affirmative: She studies English. / They study English.
   Negative: She doesn't study English. / They don't study English.
4. Affirmative: He does the laundry. / We do the laundry.
   Negative: He doesn't do the laundry. / We don't do the laundry.
5. Affirmative: She has breakfast. / They have breakfast.
   Negative: She doesn't have breakfast. / They don't have breakfast.

E

1. I don't have a job.
2. This class has many students.
3. My friend doesn't like this city.
4. My husband works in New York.
5. I call my family every week.
6. My country has beautiful weather.
7. He studies hard.
8. He washes the dishes.
9. He plays soccer.
10. I do homework every day.
11. We take a test every Friday.

Have Fun Lessons 31–34: Student Book

```
                          1G   O
        2S   T   U   3D   Y         E
        T             O       4T  A   L   K   S
5P   L   A   Y       6E   A   T   S
     Y               S                7M
8H   A   S           N                I
A                9T  A   K   E   S    S
V                                     S
E                                     E
                                      S
```

Lesson 35: Student Book

A

1. Yes, he does.
2. Yes, he does.
3. I don't know.
4. Yes, he does.
5. No, he doesn't.
6. No, she doesn't.
7. Yes, she does.
8. I don't know.

B

Questions for Robbie:	Questions for Andy:
1. <u>Do you like</u> school?	<u>Does he like</u> school?
2. <u>Do you study</u> a lot?	<u>Does he study</u> a lot?
3. <u>Do you do</u> homework every weeknight?	<u>Does he do</u> homework every weeknight?
4. <u>Do you do</u> homework on Saturday nights?	<u>Does he do</u> homework on Saturday nights?

Lesson 36: Student Book

A

1. I <u>always</u> exercise every day.
2. I <u>usually</u> exercise around three times a week.
3. We <u>often</u> watch one or two games every day.
4. I <u>always</u> go jogging in the afternoon.
5. I <u>never</u> go jogging.
6. You <u>sometimes</u> go jogging.
7. I <u>rarely</u> go jogging.
8. Well, we're <u>always</u> busy, that's for sure!

B

1. <u>always exercise</u>   before
2. <u>usually exercise</u>   before
3. <u>often watch</u>   before
4. <u>always go</u>   before
5. <u>never go</u>   before
6. <u>sometimes go</u>   before
7. <u>rarely go</u>   before
8. <u>are always</u>   after

C
1. Simona <u>always goes</u> jogging on Thursday afternoons.
2. She <u>often/sometimes goes</u> swimming on Tuesdays.
3. She <u>never goes</u> swimming on Mondays.
4. She <u>never plays</u> volleyball on Thursdays.
5. She <u>usually works</u> at the sports center on Sundays.
6. She <u>often/sometimes watches</u> football on Monday nights.
7. She <u>never plays</u> football on Friday nights.
8. She <u>usually plays</u> tennis on Saturday mornings.

Lesson 37: Student Book

A
A. 4, B. 3, C, 6, D. 1, E. 2, F. 5

B
1. We <u>want to have</u> a big wedding.
2. They <u>need to buy</u> a wedding cake.
3. Judy's mom <u>doesn't like to take</u> pictures.
4. Judy <u>needs to get</u> a haircut.
5. Judy's parents <u>have to pay</u>.
6. They <u>don't want to have</u> problems.

Lesson 38: Student Book

A
1. At 7:00.
2. Toast.
3. My sister.
4. At 8:10.
5. Yes, it does.
6. I study and work.
7. Yes, a little.
8. In the evening.
9. In my neighborhood.
10. I want to be a doctor.

B
1. What time do you get up?
2. Do you eat breakfast?
3. What do you eat for breakfast?
4. Do you work?
5. Why do you study English?
6. Do you go to school?
7. What do you study?
8. When do you go home?
9. Do you make dinner?
10. What time do you have dinner?
11. Who do you have dinner with?
12. Where do you do your homework?

A

A: What do you usually do on weekends?
B: I stay home and sleep.
A: Do you like to go to the movies?
B: Yes. I love to go to the movies!

B

1. <u>Do</u> you live in the U.S.?
2. <u>Does</u> your teacher give a lot of homework?
3. <u>Does</u> this school have a computer lab?
4. <u>Do</u> the students in this class study hard?
5. <u>Do</u> these exercises help you learn grammar?
6. <u>Does</u> this classroom have a TV?
7. <u>Do</u> you like to do grammar exercises?
8. <u>Does</u> your teacher speak your first language?

D

1. I like to study English.
2. What time does he go to school?
3. Does your sister live in the U.S.?
4. Where do you live?
5. What time does your class begin?
6. I want to study English.
7. My husband needs to work hard.
8. When do you go to work?
9. Does your father speak English?
10. She has to work after school.

E

1. Where do you live?
2. Where do your parents live?
3. Where do you work?
4. Where does your husband work?
5. Do you have children?
6. How old is your son?
7. What time does your class start?
8. What time does your class end?

Have Fun Lessons 35–38: Student Book

A Word Search

Adverbs of Frequency	Nouns	Verbs
always	homework	make
rarely	class	need
sometimes	dinner	take
never	football	have
often	guitar	want

```
W  K  M  A  K  E  P  F  T  L
A  I  R  A  L  W  A  Y  S  L
N  O  R  O  F  T  E  N  A
T  V  N  A  W  F  I  N  M  B
W  R  L  D  R  E  E  D  U  T
S  E  M  I  T  E  M  O  S  O
S  V  T  N  D  C  L  O  W  O
A  E  A  N  A  W  S  Y  H  F
L  N  K  E  R  A  T  I  U  G
C  O  E  R  E  V  A  H  I  C
```

Lesson 39: Student Book

A

_T_ 1. The TV reporter is at a job fair.
_F_ 2. The job fair is outside.
_T_ 3. The reporter is talking to people at the fair.
_T_ 4. Many people are looking for jobs.
_F_ 5. Pablo is a high school student.
_F_ 6. Paula is looking for a job.
_T_ 7. Paula is giving information to people at the fair.
_T_ 8. The fair is noisy because people are talking.
_F_ 9. Everyone is wearing a suit.
_T_ 10. Everyone is walking around.

B

1. It <u>is raining</u>.
2. Many people <u>are looking</u> for jobs.
3. The reporter <u>is holding</u> a microphone.
4. The reporter <u>is wearing</u> a suit.
5. Pablo <u>is wearing</u> blue jeans.
6. The reporter <u>is looking</u> at Paula.
7. Paula <u>is talking</u> to the reporter.
8. Paula <u>is listening</u> to the reporter's questions.
9. Many people <u>are talking</u>.
10. They <u>are talking</u> about jobs.
11. They <u>are walking</u> around the gym.
12. A young man <u>is talking</u> on a cell phone.

C

1. Pablo is wearing blue jeans.
2. People are talking.
3. Paula is standing.
4. The reporter is working.
5. It's raining./It is raining.
6. They are looking for jobs.
7. She is wearing a suit.
8. He is talking on a cell phone.
9. People are asking questions.
10. A man is answering questions.

A

It's 11:30 and <u>I'm reporting</u> from Times Square in New York City. It's very cold. The temperature is about 25 degrees. <u>We're waiting</u> for midnight, and <u>we're having</u> a great time. Everyone <u>is wearing</u> warm winter clothes. Some bands <u>are playing</u> music, and people <u>are dancing</u>. They <u>are trying</u> to stay warm. A lot of people <u>are making</u> noise. Some people <u>are smiling</u> and <u>carrying</u> big Happy New Year signs. And some people <u>are sitting</u> down and <u>drinking</u> hot coffee. Maybe they're tired. Some people <u>are eating</u> ice cream cones. And it's so cold!

B

Verbs with -ing	Base Forms Of Verbs	Rule Number
1. reporting	report	1
2. waiting	wait	1
3. having	have	2
4. wearing	wear	1
5. playing	play	1/4
6. dancing	dance	2
7. trying	try	1/4
8. making	make	2
9. smiling	smile	2
10. carrying	carry	1/4
11. sitting	sit	3
12. drinking	drink	1
13. eating	eat	1/4

C

1. looking
2. celebrating
3. enjoying
4. listening
5. having
6. carrying
7. crying
8. sitting
9. ringing
10. answering
11. walking
12. giving
13. sleeping
14. running
15. playing
16. hugging

Lesson 41: Student Book

A

	Wednesday night	Friday night
1. a. Mrs. Miller is reading the newspaper.	✓	
b. Mrs. Miller isn't reading the newspaper.		✓
2. a. She isn't playing cards.	✓	
b. She is playing cards.		✓
3. a. David isn't working on the computer.		✓
b. David is working on the computer.	✓	
4. a. Jon and Pam are doing their homework.	✓	
b. Jon and Pam aren't doing their homework.		✓
5. a. Jon and Pam aren't watching TV.	✓	
b. Jon and Pam are watching TV.		✓

C

1. It isn't eating.
2. It isn't flying.
3. It isn't ringing.
4. It isn't raining.
5. It isn't working.

Lesson 42: Student Book

A

1. Yes, he is.
2. No, she isn't.
3. No, they aren't.
4. No, it isn't.

B

1. Is Jerry waking up?	Yes, he is.
2. Is Jerry smiling?	No, he isn't./No, he's not.
3. Is Sue sitting down?	No, she isn't./No, she's not.
4. Is Sue standing?	Yes, she is.
5. Are Nick and Alex riding bikes?	No, they're not./No, they aren't.
6. Are Nick and Alex swimming?	Yes, they are.
7. Is it raining in London?	Yes, it is.
8. Is it snowing in London?	No, it isn't./No, it's not.

C

1. Am I wearing the right clothes?	No, you aren't./No, you're not.
2. Am I making too much noise?	Yes, you are.
3. Are we going too fast?	Yes, we are/Yes, you are.
4. Are you studying English right now?	Yes, I am.

Lesson 43: Student Book

A

1. d
2. f
3. a
4. b
5. c
6. e

B

1. What is the babysitter doing?
2. What is the baby doing?
3. What is Janie doing?
4. What is Janie wearing?
5. What are the twins doing?
6. What are the twins wearing?

C

1. a. <u>She's holding</u> the baby.
    b. <u>She's giving</u> the baby a bottle.
    c. <u>She's sitting</u> in a rocking chair.
2. <u>She's drinking</u>.
3. <u>She's sleeping</u>.

4. <u>She's wearing</u> pajamas.
5. <u>They're watching</u> TV.
6. <u>They're wearing</u> pajamas.

D
1. Who is crying?
2. Why is she crying?
3. Who's watching TV?
4. Where are the parents going?/Where are Emily and Rick going?
5. Why are they going to the movies?
6. When are they coming home?
7. How are the children?

Review Lessons 39–43: Student Book

A
A: What are you doing?
B: I'm making dinner.
A: What are you cooking?
B: I'm cooking chicken and rice.

B
1. eating
2. taking
3. using
4. studying
5. playing
6. having
7. running
8. staying
9. sitting
10. driving
11. coming
12. stopping

C
1. Mrs. Miller <u>is reading</u> the newspaper.
2. She <u>is sitting</u> on the couch.
3. She <u>is drinking</u> a cup of tea.
4. The children <u>are watching</u> TV.
5. They <u>are laughing</u> because it's a funny program.
6. They <u>are wearing</u> pajamas.
7. Mr. Miller <u>is working</u> on the computer.
8. Listen! The baby <u>is crying</u>.
9. The weather is bad. It <u>is raining</u> outside.
10. The cat <u>is sleeping</u> on the couch.

D
1. It <u>is/isn't raining</u> now.
2. We <u>are/aren't doing</u> an exercise in the grammar book.
3. We <u>are/aren't taking</u> a test right now.
4. The teacher <u>is/isn't writing</u> on the blackboard right now.
5. The teacher <u>is/isn't wearing</u> a sweater.
6. The teacher <u>is/isn't sitting</u> down right now. The teacher <u>is/isn't standing</u> up.
7. The students in this room <u>are/aren't sitting</u> in a circle.
8. I <u>am/am not wearing</u> a watch right now.
9. I <u>am/am not wearing</u> jeans.
10. Many students in this class <u>are/aren't wearing</u> jeans.

E

1. Mother: Hi! How <u>are you doing</u>?
2. Daughter: <u>We're doing</u> fine. How about you?
3. Mother: I'm fine. What <u>are the children doing</u>?
4./5. Daughter: <u>Susan is checking</u> her e-mail and <u>the boys are playing</u> soccer.
6. Mother: <u>Is the baby sleeping</u>?
7./8. Daughter: No. <u>I'm holding</u> him now because <u>he's crying</u>!
9. Mother: I hear him now....Oh, how's the weather? <u>Is it raining</u>?
10. Daughter: Yes, it is. <u>It's raining</u> very hard!

Have Fun Lessons 39–43: Student Book

A

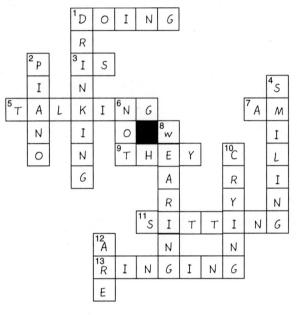

Lesson 44: Student Book

A

Routine

Every day Maggie <u>gets up</u> early. She <u>gets dressed</u>, and then she <u>goes</u> to the park. She <u>walks</u> for an hour with a friend. Then she <u>goes</u> back home and <u>takes</u> a shower. She <u>eats</u> breakfast, and then she <u>puts on</u> her uniform. She <u>works</u> in a hospital three times a week.

Routine

James <u>wakes up</u> every day around 8:00. He <u>exercises</u>, and then he <u>takes</u> a shower. He <u>eats</u> toast and fruit for breakfast. Then he <u>reads</u> the newspaper. Around 11:00, he <u>drives</u> to a homeless shelter. He <u>works</u> there every weekday for two hours. He <u>serves</u> lunch.

Right Now

Right now, Maggie and James <u>are getting</u> married. Maggie <u>is wearing</u> a beautiful dress. She <u>is holding</u> flowers. James <u>is wearing</u> a nice suit. They <u>are standing</u> together and <u>holding</u> hands. They <u>are smiling</u>.

B

Routine		Right Now
gets up	works	are getting married
gets (dressed)	wakes up	is wearing
goes (to the park)	exercises	is holding
walks (for an hour)	takes (a shower)	is wearing
goes (back home)	eats (toast and fruit)	are standing
takes (a shower)	reads (the newspaper)	are holding
eats (breakfast)	drives	are smiling
puts on (her uniform)	works	
	serves (lunch)	

C

_R_ 1. Maggie <u>gets dressed</u> early every morning.
_N_ 2. She <u>is getting dressed</u> right now.
_R_ 3. She <u>puts on</u> her uniform after breakfast.
_R_ 4. She <u>doesn't wear</u> her uniform every day.
_N_ 5. She <u>isn't wearing</u> her uniform right now.
_N_ 6. Right now, Maggie <u>is getting</u> married to James.
_N_ 7. They <u>are smiling</u> because they are happy today.
_N_ 8. <u>Are</u> they <u>smiling</u> right now?
_N_ 9. <u>Is</u> James <u>working</u> right now?

Lesson 45: Student Book

A

1. Yes, I do.
2. Yes, I do.
3. No, I'm not.
4. Yes, I do.
5. Yes, she does.
6. Yes, they do.
7. Yes, they are.
8. Yes, they are.

B

1. <u>BE—noun</u>
2. <u>BE—Place</u>
3. <u>BE—PCT</u>
4. <u>DO—verb</u>
5. <u>DO—verb</u>
6. <u>BE—PCT</u>
7. <u>DO—verb</u>
8. <u>BE—Place</u>
9. <u>BE—Place</u>
10. <u>DO—verb</u>
11. <u>BE—Adjective</u>
12. <u>BE—PCT</u>
13. <u>DO—verb</u>

C

  4. Does your teacher <u>give</u> homework?

  5. Do you <u>do</u> your homework?

  7. Do they <u>work</u> hard every day?

10. Do you <u>come</u> from Europe?

13. Do you <u>like</u> ice cream?

Lesson 46: Student Book

A

  1. They (can't) drive a car.

  2. They (can) fly and they (can) walk.

  3. They (can't) swim.

  4. The children (can) play tennis, but they (can't) play basketball.

  5. The girl (can) play the violin.

  6. They (can't) use computers.

  7. They (can) speak many languages, but they (can't) read or write.

  8. Their dog (can) read.

  9. It also (can) write.

10. They (can't) fix their spaceship.

B

	Can	**Can't**
Marty from Mars	fly	swim
Eddie from Earth	fly a kite	fly
Margie from Mars	play violin and guitar	play piano
Annie from Earth	speak English, Chinese and Spanish	understand the Martian language

C

1. I can speak English.

2. She can speak four languages.

3. We can't speak English, but we can speak Vietnamese.

4. We can speak English, and we can speak Vietnamese.

5. You can speak English very well.

Lesson 47: Student Book

A

1. No, he can't.	5. Yes, they can.
2. No, he can't.	6. No, they can't.
3. Yes, he can.	7. No, they can't.
4. No, he can't.	8. Yes, they can.

B

Please answer the following questions.

1. Can you play sports? <u>Yes, I can. I can play tennis, basketball, volleyball, baseball and soccer.</u>

2. <u>Can you</u> play musical instruments? <u>Yes, I can. I can play the piano and drums.</u>

3. <u>Can you</u> sing? <u>No, I can't.</u>

4. <u>Can you</u> draw? <u>No, I can't.</u>

5. <u>Can you</u> work with young children? <u>Yes, I can. I baby-sit a lot.</u>

6. <u>Can you</u> teach children about nature? <u>Yes, I can. I know a lot about nature.</u>

A

Right now I'm sitting in my classroom. I'm wearing jeans and a sweater because it's cold today. I always wear a sweater in the winter.

C

1. Do	6. Does	11. Are
2. Are	7. Is	12. Are
3. Do	8. Is	13. Do
4. Are	9. Do	14. Is
5. Does	10. Are	15. Does

D

Present Tense		Present Continous Tense	
Affirmative	**Negative**	**Affirmative**	**Negative**
1. He studies.	He doesn't study.	He's studying.	He isn't studying.
2. I work.	I don't work.	I'm working.	I'm not working.
3. You smoke.	You don't smoke.	You're smoking.	You aren't smoking.
4. She cries.	She doesn't cry.	She's crying.	She isn't crying.
5. He watches TV.	He doesn't watch TV.	He's watching TV.	He isn't watching TV.
6. We run.	We don't run.	We're running.	We aren't running.

E

Affirmative	Negative	Question
They can speak English.	They can't speak English.	Can they speak English?
He can play guitar.	He can't play guitar.	Can he play guitar?
She can play piano.	She can't play piano.	Can she play piano?
They can dance.	They can't dance.	Can they dance?
We can go home.	We can't go home.	Can we go home?

Have Fun Lessons 44–47: Student Book

A

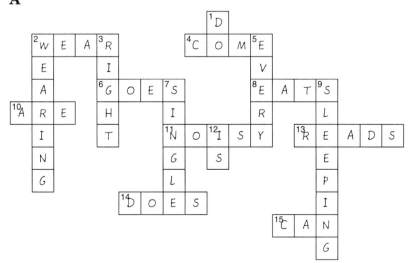

Lesson 48: Student Book

A. 2, B. 4, C. 1, D. 3

B
1. Norma and Rick were at a restaurant.
2. It was their anniversary.
3. It wasn't Norma's birthday.
4. Norma was beautiful in her black dress.
5. Rick was handsome in his new suit.
6. They were at a window table.
7. They weren't near the kitchen.
8. There were flowers on the table.
9. The food was delicious.
10. It wasn't cheap, but it wasn't very expensive.
11. The waiter was very friendly.
12. There was nice music.
13. There weren't many people there.
14. It was a very special evening.

Lesson 49: Student Book

A
1. Yes, he was.
2. Yes, he was.
3. Yes, he was.
4. Married.
5. No, she wasn't.
6. Yes, she was.
7. In Los Angeles.
8. No, they weren't.
9. Yes, he was.

B
1. Was she happy?
   Yes, she was.
2. Was their house big?
   Yes, it was.
3. Was she divorced?
   No, she wasn't.
4. Were they in an office?
   No, they weren't.
5. Were they poor?
   No, they weren't.
6. Was he a doctor?
   No, he wasn't.

C
1. She was happy.
2. She was married.
3. They were rich.
4. It was big.
5. They were at their pool.
6. He was a musician.

Lesson 50: Student Book

A
1. Laura.
2. In Mexico.
3. Last week.
4. Wonderful.
5. Two weeks.
6. Her children.
7. No, they weren't.
8. Laura was.
9. Lin was.
10. No, she wasn't.

B

1. Were you born in the U.S.?
2. Where were you born?
3. When were you born?
4. Where were you last weekend?
5. How was your weekend?
6. Were you at school yesterday?
7. Why were you at school?
8. How long were you at school last Monday?

Lesson 51: Student Book

A

In 1990, I <u>was</u> in Korea, my native country. I <u>was</u> single and I <u>was</u> a student. My friends <u>were</u> students, too. We <u>were</u> together all the time. Now I'<u>m</u> in the United States. I'<u>m</u> not single. I'<u>m</u> married. My wife and I <u>are</u> always together. We'<u>re</u> both lawyers and we'<u>re</u> very busy. But we <u>are</u> with our friends on weekends.

A long time ago, my husband and I <u>were</u> rich. We <u>were</u> famous movie stars in Hollywood. Now life <u>is</u> different. We'<u>re</u> not married and we'<u>re</u> not rich. And we'<u>re</u> not famous! I'<u>m</u> in Toronto, and my ex-husband <u>is</u> in Dallas. I'<u>m</u> a restaurant owner, and he'<u>s</u> a teacher. I'm happy, and he <u>is</u>, too!

B

1. was, is
2. was, is
3. was, was, is
4. was, was, is
5. were, were, aren't
6. is, wasn't
7. weren't, were, are

C

Jerry: Yesterday, I was in the city. I was with my friend Elaine. We were at a nice restaurant. The food was good, but it wasn't cheap.

Elaine: I am with Jerry. We aren't at school. We are at my house. Jerry and my dad are in the garden. My mother and I are in the kitchen. My sister isn't home.

Review Lessons 48–51: Student Book

A

Last Saturday I was in the city. I was with my friend. We were at a nice restaurant. The food was good, but it wasn't cheap.

B

My life <u>is</u> very different today. Five years ago, I <u>was</u> in my country. My life <u>was</u> hard, but my parents <u>were</u> near me. Now I <u>am</u> in the U.S., and my parents <u>are</u> far away. Five years ago I <u>was</u> single. I <u>was</u> a teacher in my country. Now I <u>am</u> married. My wife <u>is</u> American. We <u>are</u> both students. We have a son. Our son <u>was</u> born last year. Now he <u>is</u> almost one year old!

D

1. How was the party?
2. Where was the party?
3. When was the party?
4. How long was the party?

5. How was the food?
6. How was the music?
7. Were you tired?

E

1. I was born in Mexico.
2. My children were born in the U.S.
3. They weren't born in Mexico.
4. Where were you yesterday?
5. How long was your vacation?
6. Was the test difficult?
7. My sister was sick last night.
8. The children were late for school.
9. Where were the students last night?
10. I wasn't absent yesterday.
11. I liked the movie. It was interesting.

Have Fun Lessons 48–51: Student Book

A

Various answers are possible.

B

Answers for Student A

John F. Kennedy; an American president; 1920; the U.S.
Simon Bolivar; an explorer; 1532; Spain
Marie Curie; a scientist; 1867; Poland

Answers for Student B

Frida Kahlo, a painter; 1907; Mexico
Mao Tse-tung; a political leader; 1893; China
Cleopatra; a queen; 200; Egypt

Lesson 52: Student Book

A

Greetings from Acapulco. I'm visiting my family in Mexico. I <u>arrived</u> yesterday afternoon. My sister and I <u>walked</u> around our neighborhood on Saturday morning and we <u>talked</u> for two hours. I <u>was</u> interested in all the news. My mom <u>cooked</u> a special dinner, and after dinner we <u>watched</u> family videos.

It <u>was</u> fun. Today I'm tired. I need to rest.

I hope everything is fine in San Fransico!

Take care,
    Jose

B

1. brushed
2. washed
3. shaved
4. combed
5. cooked
6. cleaned
7. watered
8. ironed
9. mailed
10. exercised
11. finished
12. started
13. painted
14. walked
15. called
16. visited
17. rented
18. listened
19. danced
20. enjoyed

C

Five years ago, Jose was a student at the City College of San Francisco. He wanted to be a doctor and he needed to take many science classes. He liked his classes. In his free time, he played soccer with his friends. His family was in Mexico, and he sometimes visited them.

Lesson 53: Student Book

B

2	1. Jose <u>danced</u> all night at a club.
1	2. He <u>visited</u> his friends for three hours.
3	3. He <u>sipped</u> cold drinks on the beach.
1/4	4. He <u>played</u> soccer with his cousins.
1	5. They <u>talked to</u> him in the evening.
1	6. His sister <u>showed</u> him pictures of their family.
3	7. He <u>hugged</u> his mother a lot.
1/4	8. He <u>stayed</u> home when the weather was bad.
1/3	9. He <u>fixed</u> his father's stereo.
4	10. He <u>carried</u> groceries for his mom.
2	11. He <u>smiled</u> a lot because he was happy.
1	12. When his vacation <u>ended</u>, he wasn't happy.

C

Base Form	Number of Syllables	—ED Form	Number of Syllables
1. dance	1	danced	1
2. visit	2	visited	3
3. sip	1	sipped	1
4. play	1	played	1
5. talk	1	talked	1
6. show	1	showed	1
7. hug	1	hugged	1
8. stay	1	stayed	1
9. fix	1	fixed	1
10. carry	2	carried	2
11. smile	1	smiled	1
12. end	1	ended	2

Lesson 54: Student Book

A

Last Saturday morning, Annie <u>went</u> shopping. She <u>bought</u> lettuce, tomatoes, a cucumber, an onion, and carrots. In the evening, at around 6:30, her husband, Joe, <u>made</u> a big salad. He washed and <u>cut</u> the vegetables. Then he <u>put</u> them into a salad bowl. Annie <u>made</u> her special salad dressing with oil and vinegar, and she <u>put</u> it into a jar. She also picked some beautiful flowers from her garden and <u>made</u> a bouquet.

At around 7:00, they <u>got</u> into their car. They <u>took</u> the salad and the bouquet, and they <u>drove</u> to their friend Ken's house for a potluck dinner. They parked near Ken's house. When they <u>got</u> out of their car, they <u>heard</u> music. Annie <u>rang</u> the bell and Ken <u>came</u> to the door. Annie and Joe <u>gave</u> him the bouquet and he smiled and <u>said</u>, "Thank you! Are the flowers from your garden? They're beautiful!" Then he <u>said</u>, "Thanks for the salad. You can put it on the table over there."

Joe <u>put</u> the salad on the table. He <u>put</u> the dressing on the salad. Then he(mixed) the salad with two long spoons. Annie(asked)him to dance. They <u>had</u> a great time at the party.

B

Regular Past Verbs			
Base Form	**Past Form**	**Base Form**	**Past Form**
1. wash	washed	4. smile	smiled
2. pick	picked	5. mix	mixed
3. park	parked	6. ask	asked

Irregular Past Verbs			
Base Form	**Past Form**	**Base Form**	**Past Form**
1. go	went	8. drive	drove
2. buy	bought	9. hear	heard
3. make	made	10. ring	rang
4. cut	cut	11. come	came
5. put	put	12. give	gave
6. get	got	13. say	said
7. take	took	14. have	had

C
1. went
2. put
3. made
4. wore
5. went
6. sat
7. drank
8. ate
9. read
10. took

Lesson 55: Student Book

A

A. weekend, B. weekday, C. weekday
D. weekend, E. weekday, F. weekend

B
1. Jeff didn't go to work on Sunday.
   He studied and watched TV on Sunday.
2. Jeff didn't sleep late on Tuesday.
   He slept late on Sunday./He got up early on Tuesday.
3. Jeff didn't do his laundry on Monday.
   He did his laundry on Saturday.
4. Jeff didn't go out to dinner Sunday night.
   He went out to dinner on Friday night.
5. Jeff didn't do his homework on Saturday.
   He did his homework on Monday, Tuesday, Wednesday, and Thursday.

6. Jeff didn't get up early on Sunday.
   He got up early on Monday, Tuesday, Wednesday, and Thursday./He slept late on Sunday.
7. Jeff didn't go to school on Saturday.
   He went to school on the weekdays.

Lesson 56: Student Book

A

Last summer, I <u>wasn't</u> here. I traveled, but I <u>wasn't</u> a tourist. I was in my native country. I <u>didn't</u> speak English. I spoke my native language. I <u>didn't</u> go to school and I <u>didn't</u> go to work. I relaxed. I <u>wasn't</u> tired. I had a vacation. I was very happy. But I missed my brother, Thomas. We <u>weren't</u> together. He <u>didn't</u> come with me.

Last summer, I <u>didn't</u> have a vacation. I <u>didn't</u> go to my native country. I was here. But my sister and parents <u>weren't</u> here. I stayed here and studied English. In the afternoons and evenings I worked. I was a taxi driver. I <u>didn't</u> have time to go to the beach. I <u>didn't</u> relax. I was very busy and I was very tired. But I was happy.

B

WASN'T / WEREN'T			DIDN'T
With Nouns a tourist	**With Adjectives** tired together	**With Places** here	**With Verbs** speak go come have relax

C

1. Tina <u>didn't</u> work last summer.
2. She <u>didn't</u> get up early.
3. She <u>wasn't</u> busy or tired.
4. She <u>didn't</u> go shopping.
5. She <u>wasn't</u> in the U.S.
6. Thomas <u>wasn't</u> in his native country.
7. He <u>didn't</u> have free time.
8. He <u>didn't</u> take naps.
9. He <u>wasn't</u> relaxed.
10. Tina and Thomas <u>weren't</u> together.
11. They <u>didn't</u> take a trip together.
12. They <u>didn't</u> see each other.

D

Last summer, Tina visited her family in China. She didn't go to school and she didn't work. She didn't want to be far from her family for a long time. She was relaxed in China, but she wasn't relaxed in the U.S. Thomas didn't go back to China. He didn't have time. He didn't want to stop his classes in the summer.

Review Lessons 52–56: Student Book

A

I was born in Brazil. I arrived in New York ten years ago. I didn't like it here because everything was very expensive, but now I like it here.

C

EVERY DAY		YESTERDAY	
Affirmative	**Negative**	**Affirmative**	**Negative**
I'm tired.	I'm not tired.	I was tired.	I wasn't tired.
I work hard.	I don't work hard.	I worked hard.	I didn't work hard.
He plays soccer.	He doesn't play soccer.	He played soccer.	He didn't play soccer.
You are busy.	You aren't busy.	You were busy.	You weren't busy.
They study hard.	They don't study hard.	They studied hard.	They didn't study hard.

D

Rule 1	Rule 2	Rule 3	Rule 4
started ✓	danced	shopped	cried
walked	liked	hugged	carried
needed ✓	loved	stopped	tried
wanted ✓	smiled	sipped	studied

E

1. I didn't study last night.
2. I stayed home yesterday.
3. The girl liked her present.
4. He washed the dishes last night.
5. I worked in Texas last year.
6. You didn't work last night.
7. He played tennis two days ago.
8. I needed to work.
9. They were happy last year.
10. I was tired last night.
11. She took two classes last year.
12. We didn't play baseball yesterday afternoon.
13. We ate dinner at 8:00 last night.
14. We weren't busy yesterday.
15. The baby slept ten hours yesterday.

Have Fun Lessons 52–56: Student Book

A

Base Form	Past Form	Base Form	Past Form	Base Form	Past Form
carry	carried	go	went	smile	smiled
drink	drank	make	made	stop	stopped
eat	ate	play	played	study	studied
get	got	put	put	take	took
give	gave	read	read	wear	wore

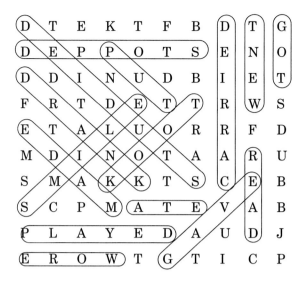

Lesson 57: Student Book

A

1. <u>Was</u> the New Year's Eve party fun? Yes, it <u>was</u>.
2. <u>Was</u> the party at Sam's house? No, it <u>wasn't</u>.
3. <u>Was</u> Sam home at 2:00 a.m.? No, he <u>wasn't</u>.
4. <u>Did</u> Sam have dinner there? Yes, he <u>did</u>.
5. <u>Was</u> the food good? Yes, it <u>was</u>.
6. <u>Did</u> his friends dance? Yes, they <u>did</u>.
7. <u>Were</u> they quiet? No, they <u>weren't</u>.
8. <u>Did</u> they shake hands at midnight? No, they <u>didn't</u>.

B

1. <u>Was</u> Thanksgiving last Thursday? <u>Yes, it was.</u>
2. <u>Did</u> Mike eat with his family? <u>Yes, he did.</u>
3. <u>Was</u> the food terrible? <u>No, it wasn't.</u>
4. <u>Did</u> Mike and his sister take a walk? <u>Yes, they did.</u>
5. <u>Were</u> they tired on Thursday night? <u>Yes, they were.</u>
6. <u>Did</u> they wash the dishes on Thursday night? <u>No, they didn't.</u>
7. <u>Did</u> Mike clean the house on Friday? <u>Yes, he did.</u>
8. <u>Did</u> Mike go to work on Friday? <u>No, he didn't.</u>
9. <u>Was</u> Mike at work on Friday? <u>No, he wasn't.</u>
10. <u>Was</u> Mike's weekend good? <u>Yes, it was.</u>

C

1. <u>Did</u> you celebrate with your family?
2. <u>Were</u> you busy before the holiday?
3. <u>Did</u> you wear special clothes?
4. <u>Were</u> you happy?
5. <u>Did</u> you eat special food?
6. <u>Was</u> the food delicious?
7. <u>Did</u> you dance?
8. <u>Did</u> you stay home?
9. <u>Did</u> you go out?
10. <u>Were</u> you tired after the holiday?

A

1. <u>Who</u> did Josh have brunch with on Sunday morning?
2. <u>Why</u> did he go to the ATM?
3. <u>Where</u> did he play soccer?
4. <u>Who</u> did he have dinner with?
5. <u>What</u> did he do on Saturday afternoon?
6. <u>What time</u> did he go to Gary and Linda's wedding?
7. <u>How</u> did he get there?
8. <u>Where</u> did he study?
9. <u>When</u> did he clean his apartment?

B

1. Where did Josh and his mother eat?
2. What time did they have brunch?
3. When did Josh play soccer?
4. How did Josh get to Kennedy Field?
5. Who did Josh go to the movies with?
6. Why did he study?
7. Where did he go on Friday night?

Lesson 59: Student Book

Answers may vary.

Lesson 60: Student Book

A

Thirty years ago, Ricky <u>was</u>^{past} a quiet child. He <u>was</u>^{past} very shy. He <u>didn't talk</u>^{past} in school. He <u>stayed</u>^{past} next to his mother all the time.

When Ricky <u>was</u>^{past} a teenager, he <u>went</u>^{past} to the movies every Saturday. He <u>wanted</u>^{past} to be a movie star. He <u>wasn't</u>^{past} shy. He <u>performed</u>^{past} in school plays. He <u>was</u>^{past} very good-looking.

When he <u>was</u>^{past} 25, he <u>got</u>^{past} married. When he <u>was</u>^{past} 29, he <u>got</u>^{past} divorced. He <u>has</u>^{pres} two children, a boy and a girl.

Today he <u>is</u>^{pres} very famous. He <u>is</u>^{pres} on TV almost every day. He always <u>smiles</u>^{pres} and <u>talks</u>^{pres} to people. He <u>has</u>^{pres} a beautiful girlfriend, but he <u>doesn't want</u>^{pres} to get married.

Right now he <u>is flying</u>^{pc} to New York. He <u>is reading</u>^{pc} a magazine story about his new movie. He<u>'s looking</u>^{pc} at his picture and he<u>'s smiling</u>^{pc}. He <u>can't believe</u>^{pres} that he<u>'s</u>^{pres} the boy who <u>was</u>^{past} shy and quiet 30 years ago.

C

Ricky's sister, Patricia, <u>is</u> also famous. She <u>is</u> a singer. She <u>gives</u> concerts all over the world. Every day she <u>flies</u> to different cities. She <u>has</u> a lot of money.

Life <u>was</u> different 30 years ago when she <u>was</u> a child. She <u>was</u> poor. She <u>didn't have</u> money. Her mother and father <u>worked</u> six days a week. She <u>slept</u> in a room with Ricky and their two sisters. Patricia <u>had</u> one pair of shoes and one dress. But she <u>wasn't</u> hungry. Her parents <u>had</u> money for food.

When she <u>was</u> a child, she <u>was</u> poor. But she <u>was</u> happy. Her family <u>loved</u> her, and she <u>loved</u> her family.

Right now, Patricia <u>is driving</u> her car in New York. She <u>is going</u> to the airport. She <u>is listening</u> to the radio and she <u>is singing</u>. She <u>is</u> happy—her brother <u>is coming</u> to visit her.

Review Lessons 57–60: Student Book

A

A: Where were you last night? Were you sick?
B: No, I was with my brother. He's visiting me. He lives in New York.
A: What did you do?
B: We had dinner.

B

1. What <u>are</u> you <u>doing</u> now? (present continuous)
2. We're <u>doing</u> this exercise. (present continuous)
3. What <u>did</u> you <u>do</u> last night? (past)
4. We <u>didn't do</u> anything. (past)
5. <u>Were</u> you sick? (past)
6. No, we <u>were</u> tired. (past)
7. <u>Are</u> you married? (present)
8. No, but I'm <u>looking</u> for a wife. (present continuous)
9. <u>Do</u> you <u>want</u> to learn more English? (present)
10. Yes, but I <u>don't have</u> time! (present)

C

1. <u>Are you</u> tired today?
2. <u>Were you</u> tired last night?
3. <u>Are you</u> married?
4. <u>Do you</u> have any children?
5. <u>Did you</u> do your homework last night?
6. <u>Are you</u> working right now?
7. <u>Do you</u> like hamburgers?
8. <u>Are you</u> at home right now?
9. <u>Did you</u> have dinner before you came to class?
10. <u>Are you</u> wearing glasses?
11. <u>Were you</u> sick yesterday?
12. <u>Were you</u> absent from class last week?

D

STATEMENTS:

Present	Present Continuous	Past
They work hard.	They are working hard.	They worked hard.
He studies hard.	He is studying hard.	He studied hard.
It rains in May.	It is raining.	It rained yesterday.

QUESTIONS:

Present	Present Continuous	Past
Do they work hard?	Are they working hard?	Did they work hard?
Does he study hard?	Is he studying hard?	Did he study hard?
Does it rain in May?	Is it raining now?	Did it rain yesterday?

E

1. When did you come here?
2. Where do you live?
3. He worked very hard.
4. I'm not late for this class.
5. I'm never late for this class.
6. Did the class start on time?
7. Did he study English?
8. When were you born?

Have Fun Lessons 57–60: Student Book

A

1. E N J O (Y) E D
2. V (I) S I T E D
3. B (O) (U) G H T
4. C (L) E A N (E) D
5. D R (O) (V) E

Sentence: I love you.

Lesson 61: Student Book

A

1. Barbara
2. Ellen
3. Next weekend
4. For a job interview.
5. At Barbara's.

B

1. is going to go
2. is going to have
3. are going to eat
4. are going to talk
5. am going to move
6. are going to visit
7. are going to see
8. are going to have
9. is going to return
10. is going to take
11. is going to be
12. is going to rain

Lesson 62: Student Book

A

1. It isn't going to rain tomorrow.
2. It isn't going to be cold.
3. It's going to be beautiful.

4. It's going to be sunny.
5. The temperature is going to be in the 80s.
6. It isn't going to be cloudy.
7. It's going to be clear and cool tomorrow evening.
8. The low temperature is going to be in the 60s.
9. The reporter isn't going to stay home tomorrow.
10. She and her family are going to go to the beach.

B
1. They are going to get married on Saturday.
   They aren't going to get married on Sunday.
2. They are going to have a big party.
   They aren't going to have a small party.
3. Diana is going to wear a wedding gown.
   She isn't going to wear a short dress.
4. Joey is going to wear a tuxedo.
   He isn't going to wear a suit.
5. They are going to fly to Hawaii.
   They aren't going to take a boat.

Lesson 63: Student Book

A

1. Yes, they are.
2. No, they're not.
3. Yes, they are.
4. No, he isn't.
5. Yes, she is.
6. No, she isn't.
7. Yes, he is.
8. Yes, he is.
9. Yes, they are.
10. No, they're not.

B
1. Are Janet's parents going to visit?	Yes, they are.
2. Is Janet going to cook?	No, she's not.
3. Is Paul going to cook?	Yes, he is.
4. Are they going to eat out?	No, they're not.
5. Are Janet's parents going to bring presents?	Yes, they are.
6. Is Nancy going to talk to her grandmother?	Yes, she is.

C
1. <u>Are Janet and Nancy going to pick up Nancy's parents?</u>
   <u>Yes, they are.</u>
2. <u>Is the police officer going to write a ticket?</u>
   <u>Yes, he is.</u>
3. <u>Are Janet, Nancy, and Janet's parents going to tell Paul about the ticket?</u>
   <u>No, they're not.</u>

Lesson 64: Student Book

A
1. b, 2. d, 3. a, 4. c

B
1. What is Mario going to do?
2. Why is he going to move to a new apartment?
3. What is he going to rent?
4. When is he going to move?

5. Where are Tatiane and Bruno going to go?
6. Why are they going to go back to France.
7. How are they going to go?
8. Who are they going to see?/Who are they going to stay with?

Review Lessons 61–64: Student Book

A

Teacher: <u>We're going to finish this book soon!</u>
Student: <u>Are we going to take a test?</u>
Teacher: <u>Yes, I'm going to give a test next week.</u>
Student: <u>Is it going to be easy?</u>

B

1. are going to take
2. is going to close
3. am going to eat
4. is going to play
5. is going to rain
6. is going to do
7. is going to be
8. am going to go

D

1. April 16, 2005   <u>tomorrow</u>
2. April 17, 2005   <u>the day after tomorrow</u>
3. April 18, 2005   <u>in three days</u>
4. April 22, 2005   <u>next week</u>
5. May, 2005   <u>next month</u>
6. April 18, 2006   <u>next year</u>

E

What are you going to do on your vacation?
Where are you going to go?
Who are you going to go with?
Where are you going to stay?
How long are you going to stay there?
Why are you going to go there?
What time are you going to leave?
Are you going to go to bed early tonight?

Have Fun Lessons 61–64: Student Book

A

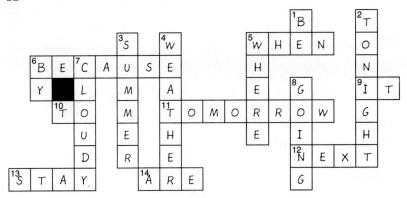

Expansion Activities Answer Key

Lesson 1: Expansion Activity

Various answers are possible.

Lesson 2: Expansion Activity

A

M ~~m~~ike	a table	P ~~p~~aris	bedrooms	H ~~h~~elen
S ~~s~~ony™	a sofa	M ~~m~~exico	D ~~d~~isneyland™	books
S W ~~s~~tar ~~w~~ars™	doors	E ~~e~~lizabeth	P ~~p~~epsi™	a kitchen

B

People	Places	Things
Mike	*Paris*	*Sony*
Helen	*Mexico*	*Star Wars*
Elizabeth	*Disneyland*	*Pepsi*

Lesson 3: Expansion Activity

Various answers are possible.

Lesson 4: Expansion Activity

A

My name (is) Anna. I (live) in Chicago. I (go) to school. At school, I (study) English. I (read) books. On Saturday and Sunday, I (sleep) Then, I (run) and (swim) I (go) to parties. I (love) Chicago!

Lesson 5: Expansion Activity

A

1. (am)
2. They('re)
3. (is)
4. (are)
5. I('m)
6. (are)
7. He('s)
8. (is)
9. You('re)
10. (are)

B

1. She is/She's a teacher.
2. We are/We're happy together.
3. I am/I'm a soccer player.
4. He is/He's at school every day.
5. You are/You're 16 years old.
6. They are/They're from Chicago.
7. I am/I'm an architect.
8. They are/They're big.
9. She is/She's tall.
10. You are/You're twins.

Lesson 6: Expansion Activity

A

My school <u>is</u> beautiful. It'<u>s</u> in a new building. The classes <u>are</u> interesting. The teachers <u>are</u> good. My teacher <u>is</u> early every day. My room <u>is</u> nice. The students <u>are</u> friendly. I <u>am</u> busy every day. I'<u>m</u> happy at my school.

B

My school isn't beautiful. It's not/It isn't in a new building. The classes aren't/are not interesting. The teachers aren't/are not good. My teacher isn't/is not early every day. My room isn't/is not nice. The students aren't/are not friendly. I'm not/ I am not busy every day. I'm not /I am not happy at my school.

Lesson 7: Expansion Activity

Various answers are possible.

Lesson 8: Expansion Activity

Various answers are possible.

Lesson 9: Expansion Activity

Various answers are possible.

Lesson 10: Expansion Activity

Various answers are possible.

Lesson 11: Expansion Activity

Various answers are possible.

Lesson 12: Expansion Activity

A

1. That's a great street entertainer.
2. This is a really good restaurant.
3. This is a big supermarket.
4. That's a nice school.
5. This is a large tree.
6. That's a large statue.
7. This is the library.
8. This is a beautiful park.
9. That's City Hall.
10. That's a bank.

Lesson 13: Expansion Activity

A

1. Those are my shoes.
2. These are my books.
3. These are my pillows.
4. Those are great entertainers!
5. These are big trees.
6. Those are my sisters.
7. These are beautiful flowers.
8. Those are ugly statues.
9. These are my grandparents.
10. Those are my parents.

Lesson 14: Expansion Activity

A

Look at (this) picture. It's my bedroom. Over there is my closet. (That's) my shirt. (That's) my shoe. (That's) my toy. Look here on my bed. (This) is my book. (This) is my pillow. Look near the door. (That's) my sister.

B

Look at this picture. It's my bedroom. Over there is my closet. Those are my shirts. Those are my shoes. Those are my toys. Look here on my bed. These are my books. These are my pillows. Look near the door. Those are my sisters.

Lesson 15: Expansion Activity

A

Mother: Anna, (is this) your CD?
Anna: No, it's not. It's his CD.
Mother: Will, (are those) your books over there?
Will: The red book is my book. The green book is her book.
Mother: Anna, (are these) your clothes?
Anna: These are my shoes. This is his shirt.
Will: And these are my jeans.
Mother: Will, (are these) your toys?
Will: No, they aren't. They're her toys.
Mother: Anna, (is that) your watch?
Anna: Yes, it is.
Mother: Will, (is this) your ribbon?
Will: No way! That's her ribbon.

B

Anna	Will
the green book	CD
shoes	the red book
toys	shirt
watch	jeans
ribbon	

Lesson 16: Expansion Activity

A

1. What's that? It's a statue.
2. What are these? They're shoes.
3. What's this? It's a computer.
4. What's that? It's a library.
5. What are those? They're telephones.
6. What's that? It's a school.
7. What are those? They're entertainers.
8. What are these? They're headphones.
9. What's this? It's a mall.

Lesson 17: Expansion Activity

A

Anna: That's my son.
Helen: What's his name?
Anna: His name is Tom.
Helen: That's a nice name. What's his middle name?
Anna: It's Robert.
Helen: That's my daughter.
Anna: What's her name?
Helen: Robin.
Anna: What's her middle name?
Helen: Maria. We live in that house over there.
Anna: Is it the pink house?
Helen: No, it's blue.
Anna: What's the address?
Helen: It's 1411 Pine Street.
Anna: Really! We live near you. We're in that house over there.
Helen: Is it the brown house?
Anna: Yes, that's it.
Helen: What's the address?
Anna: It's 1415 Pine Street.
Helen: We're neighbors! What's your phone number?
Anna: It's 555-2579. What's your phone number?
Helen: It's 555-9752. Please call me.

B

Tom	Robin
Middle Name:	Middle Name:
Robert	Maria
Address:	Address:
1415 Pine Street	1411 Pine Street
House Color: brown	House Color: blue
Telephone Number:	Telephone Number:
555-2579	555-9752

Lesson 18: Expansion Activity

A and B

1. Where is the Eiffel Tower?	It's in Paris, France.
2. Where are the Alps?	They're in Switzerland.
3. Where is the Great Wall?	It's in China.
4. Where is the Amazon River?	It's in South America.
5. Where is Stonehenge?	It's in England./It's in Great Britain./It's in the United Kingdom.
6. Where are the Ural Mountains?	They're in Russia.
7. Where is the Statue of Liberty?	It's in New York City, the U.S.
8. Where is the Golden Gate Bridge?	It's in San Francisco, the U.S.
9. Where are the Pyramids?	They're in Egypt.
10. Where is Hollywood?	It's in California, the U.S.

Lesson 19: Expansion Activity

A

Name	Country	Nationality	First Language
Akiko	Japan	Japanese	Japanese
Maria	Mexico	Mexican	Spanish
Nguyen	Vietnam	Vietnamese	Vietnamese
Pierre	France	French	French
Andy	United States	American	English
Antonio	Brazil	Brazilian	Portuguese
Lee	China	Chinese	Chinese

B
1. Vietnam./He's from Vietnam.
2. English./His first language is English.
3. French./His nationality is French.
4. Brazil./He's from Brazil.
5. China./She's from China.
6. Spanish./Her first language is Spanish.
7. Japanese./Her nationality is Japanese.

Lesson 20: Expansion Activity

A
1. Q: What time is her English class?
   A: It's at 1:00.
2. Q: When is the basketball game?
   A: It's on Sunday.
3. Q: When is the picnic in the park?
   A: It's on Saturday.
4. Q: What time is her birthday party?
   A: It's at 6:00.
5. Q: What time is her appointment with Peter?
   A: It's at 10:00.

Lesson 21: Expansion Activity

1. ___✓___ It's sunny.
2. ___✓___ It's busy.
3. ___✓___ They're cold.
4. ___✓___ It's not very good.
5. ___✓___ I'm fine.
6. ___✓___ It's beautiful!
7. ___✓___ They're great.
8. ___✓___ She's fine.

Lesson 22: Expansion Activity

1. These shoes are expensive.
2. This computer is new.
3. That library is large.
4. Those customers are unfriendly.
5. That school is old.
6. Those T-shirts are cheap.
7. These glasses are nice.
8. This store is crowded.

Lesson 23: Expansion Activity

Various answers are possible.

Lesson 24: Expansion Activity

A

My name is Jose. I'm a student. I'm single. I am always busy at school. My sister Maria is an architect. She is always busy. She is very hardworking. Her office is in a tall building. She is single. My brother Mario is a teacher. He is funny and friendly. He is a good cook. He is married. Helen is his wife. We are all from San Francisco. I love my family.

B

	Jose	Maria	Mario
1. Who's a student?	✓		
2. Who's single?	✓	✓	
3. Who's an architect?		✓	
4. Who's a good cook?			✓
5. Who's from San Francisco?	✓	✓	✓
6. Who's friendly?			✓
7. Who is hardworking?		✓	
8. Who's always busy?	✓	✓	

Lesson 25: Expansion Activity

A
1. ___✓___ It's in February.
2. ___✓___ It's at 3:00.
3. ___✓___ It's around two hours long.

Lesson 26: Expansion Activity

A

1. They are over there.
2. There are two children in their family.
3. They are in their car.
4. Their father is over there.
5. They're with their mother.
6. There is a monkey over there.
7. Their parents aren't there.
8. There are two bedrooms in their house.
9. They're with their teacher in their school./They're in their school with their teacher.
10. Their children are there.

Lesson 27: Expansion Activity

A

John loves his family. Kathy is his ⟨mother.⟩ She is a doctor. His ⟨father's⟩ name is Joe. He's a lawyer. John's ⟨sister⟩ is Carol. She's a teacher. John has two ⟨brothers,⟩ Harry and James. Harry is an architect. James is an artist. John is married. His ⟨wife⟩ is Sue. Sue is a music teacher. John's ⟨son⟩ is Martin. Martin is a student. John's family is very big!

B

1. John is <u>Sue's</u> husband.
2. Kathy is <u>Martin's</u> grandmother.
3. Harry is <u>Sue's</u> brother-in-law.
4. Harry is <u>John's/James's</u> brother.
5. James is <u>Martin's</u> uncle.
6. Martin is <u>Joe's/Kathy's</u> grandson.
7. Carol is <u>Martin's</u> aunt.

C

1. Harry is Martin's <u>uncle</u>.
2. Martin is Carol's <u>nephew</u>.
3. James is Sue's <u>brother-in-law</u>.
4. Carol is John's <u>sister</u>.
5. Joe is Martin's <u>grandfather</u>.
6. Martin is John's <u>son</u>.
7. Martin is Kathy's <u>grandson</u>.
8. Joe's is Kathy's <u>husband</u>.

Lesson 28: Expansion Activity

A

⟨John's⟩ house is very big. There are three ⟨bedrooms⟩ and two ⟨bathrooms.⟩ ⟨John's⟩ in the house now. ⟨He's⟩ in the living room. ⟨There's⟩ a party right now. ⟨John's⟩ friends are at the party. ⟨John's⟩ happy. His ⟨friends⟩ are happy, too.

B

Possessive 's	Contracted 's	Plural s
John's	John's	bedrooms
John's	He's	bathrooms
	There's	friends
	John's	

Lesson 29: Expansion Activity

A

   Robert is a student. Every weekday, he <u>goes</u> to school at 9:00. He <u>goes</u> home at 5:00. He <u>goes</u> to bed around 11:00. On weekends, he often <u>goes</u> to the beach. Every summer, he <u>goes</u> to the mountains.

   Karen is an architect. Her office is in a tall building. Her building is downtown. Every weekday, she <u>goes</u> to work at 8:00 a.m. She <u>goes</u> home around 6:00. On Saturdays, she <u>goes</u> to the beach. On Sundays, she <u>goes</u> to the mall. Sometimes, she <u>goes</u> to the movies.

   Andy is a doctor. His office is downtown. He always <u>goes</u> to work at 9:00 a.m. On Mondays and Wednesdays, he <u>goes</u> home at 4:00. On Tuesdays, Thursdays, and Fridays, he <u>goes</u> home at 7:00. He <u>goes</u> to bed at 10:00. Every Saturday, he <u>goes</u> to the movies.

B

He or She...	Robert	Karen	Andy
...goes to school.	✓		
...goes downtown to work.		✓	✓
...goes to work at 9:00.			✓
...goes to the beach.	✓	✓	
...goes home at 5:00.	✓		
...goes to the mall on Sundays.		✓	
...goes to the movies on Saturdays.			✓
...goes to the mountains every summer.	✓		
...sometimes goes home at 4:00.			✓

Lesson 30: Expansion Activity

Various answers are possible.

Lesson 31: Expansion Activity

A

   Ann and Kim are sisters. Ann <u>gets up</u> at 6:00 every day. Kim <u>gets up</u> at 10:00. Ann <u>takes</u> a shower in the morning. Kim <u>takes</u> a shower every night. Ann <u>teaches</u> children at a school. She <u>works</u> from 8:00 to 4:00. Kim <u>works</u> in a restaurant. She<u>'s</u> a waitress. She <u>works</u> from 3:00 to 11:00. On weekends, Ann <u>rides</u> her bike in the mountains. Kim <u>goes</u> shopping at the mall. Ann and Kim <u>are</u> very different.

B
1. Kim
2. Kim
3. Ann
4. Ann
5. Kim

C

1. eat
2. rides
3. go
4. takes
5. brush
6. gets up

Lesson 32: Expansion Activity

A

1.carries   2. works   3. fixes   4. wakes up   5. goes   6. eats   7. brushes   8. gets
9. plays   10. lives   11. tries   12. writes   13. washes   14 makes   15. watches
16. takes   17. misses   18. drinks

Lesson 33: Expansion Activity

Various answers are possible.

Lesson 34: Expansion Activity

A

1. works
2. gets up
3. doesn't eat
4. doesn't drive
5. takes
6. doesn't go
7. goes
8. don't eat
9. go
10. don't go
11. take
12. go
13. play
14. plays
15. doesn't play

Lesson 35: Expansion Activity

A

1. Ben doesn't teach third grade.
   Does Ben teach third grade?
2. It doesn't rain in April.
   Does it rain in April?
3. They don't want pizza.
   Do they want pizza?
4. Carolyn doesn't like singing.
   Does Carolyn like singing?
5. You don't go to the beach on weekends.
   Do you go to the beach on weekends?
6. I'm not late for class.
   Am I late for class?

Lesson 36: Expansion Activity

1. I always play tennis on Saturdays.
2. We often go swimming in the summer.
3. She rarely plays baseball in the winter.
4. Steve is usually late for work.
5. They sometimes go to the beach on weekends./They go to the beach on week ends sometimes.
6. He always goes to school on weekdays.
7. I never go skiing with John.

Lesson 37: Expansion Activity

A

      Maria is a college student in New York City. She goes to class from Monday to Friday. She <u>has to take</u> the bus. Her classes are very difficult. She <u>needs to study</u> every day. On the weekends, Maria <u>has to work</u> in a restaurant. She doesn't <u>like to work</u> there. She <u>needs to get</u> money for school. In the summer, Maria takes a short vacation. She <u>likes to go</u> to the beach. She <u>likes to swim</u>. In the winter, she <u>likes to go</u> to the mountains. She doesn't <u>like to ski</u>. She goes ice-skating. After college, Maria <u>wants to be</u> an architect. She <u>wants to work</u> in Mexico City or Los Angeles. It's warm there. She doesn't <u>want to stay</u> in New York. It's very cold there.

B

1. true
2. false
3. false
4. true
5. false
6. false
7. true
8. false
9. true
10. true

Lesson 38: Expansion Activity

A
1. What do you do on weekends?
2. I go to the beach.
3. Where does he go to school?
4. He goes to school in Chicago.
5. Why does he have two jobs?
6. He sends money to his family.

B
1. What time does the movie start?
2. What does she do on weekends?
3. Who do you work with?
4. Where do they go in the winter?
5. When does your English course begin?
6. What time do they eat dinner?

Lesson 39: Expansion Activity

Various answers are possible.

Lesson 40: Expansion Activity

A
1. putting
2. reading
3. stopping
4. listening
5. having
6. carrying
7. eating
8. crying
9. standing
10. sitting
11. writing
12. raining
13. walking
14. working
15. giving
16. sleeping
17. running
18. dancing

Lesson 41: Expansion Activity

A
1. They aren't eating breakfast./They're not eating breakfast.
2. She's not reading a magazine./She isn't reading a magazine.
3. They're not taking a walk in the park./They aren't taking a walk in the park.
4. We're not playing cards./We aren't playing cards.
5. It's not sitting in the tree./It isn't sitting in the tree.
6. I'm not eating dinner with my friends.
7. You aren't standing on my foot./You're not standing on my foot.
8. Lou isn't writing a letter./Lou's not writing a letter.
9. It isn't snowing in the mountains./It's not snowing in the mountains.
10. Mike and Thomas aren't carrying my luggage.

Lesson 42: Expansion Activity

Various answers are possible.

Lesson 43: Expansion Activity

C
1. What are you cooking?
2. When are we going home?
3. Who is coming to the party?
4. Why is he leaving?
5. Where is your brother going?

Lesson 44: Expansion Activity

Various answers are possible.

Lesson 45: Expansion Activity

A

1. Ann doesn't eat breakfast at 8:00 every morning.
   Does Ann eat breakfast at 8:00 every morning?
2. They don't go to the mountains in the summer.
   Do they go to the mountains in the summer?
3. He's not doing the laundry./He isn't doing the laundry.
   Is he doing the laundry?
4. She's not very friendly./She isn't very friendly.
   Is she very friendly?
5. You don't visit your parents in the winter.
   Do you visit your parents in the winter?
6. We're not from San Francisco./We aren't from San Francisco.
   Are we from San Francisco?
7. He doesn't want to take a vacation.
   Does he want to take a vacation?

Lesson 46: Expansion Activity

A

1. John can speak English very well.
2. Mary can't swim.
3. We can speak Chinese and French.
4. They can't play the piano.
5. I can play basketball.
6. I can't play volleyball.
7. She can't read English.
8. They can swim and they can fly kites.
9. He can speak Chinese, but he can't speak Japanese.
10. We can't go to the mountains in the summer.

Lesson 47: Expansion Activity

A

1. No, he can't.
2. Yes, they can.
3. No, she can't.
4. Yes, they can.
5. Yes, she can.
6. No, they can't.
7. Yes, he can.
8. Yes, they can.
9. No, he can't.
10. No, she can't.
11. Yes, she can.
12. No, she can't.

Lesson 48: Expansion Activity

A

1. were	5. was
2. was	6. were
3. was	7. was
4. were	8. was

B

1. wasn't	5. weren't
2. weren't	6. weren't
3. wasn't	7. wasn't
4. wasn't	8. weren't

Lesson 49: Expansion Activity

Various answers are possible.

Lesson 50: Expansion Activity

A

1. J, 2. E, 3. A, 4. H, 5. C, 6. I, 7. K, 8. B, 9. D, 10. F, 11. G, 12. L

Lesson 51: Expansion Activity

Various answers are possible.

Lesson 52: Expansion Activity

A

Saturday and Sunday	Monday	Tuesday	Wednesday	Thursday	Friday
1/2	3	4	5	6 last Thursday	7
8/9 last weekend	10 three days ago	11 the day before yesterday	12 yesterday	13 today	14

Lesson 53: Expansion Activity

A

1. worried 2. clapped 3. smiled 4. stopped 5. married 6. sipped 7. played
8. talked 9. showed 10. hugged 11. carried 12. fixed 13. cried 14. danced
15. needed 16. wanted 17. rubbed 18. studied

Lesson 54: Expansion Activity

A

Yesterday, John <u>got up</u> at 8:00. He <u>took</u> a shower. Then, he <u>ate</u> breakfast. He <u>left</u> his house at 8:45. He <u>got</u> in his car and <u>drove</u> to work. He works in an office downtown. He is an architect. John <u>worked</u> all day. After work, he <u>went</u> to a Mexican restaurant for dinner. Then, he <u>went</u> to a movie. He <u>got</u> home around 10:00 and <u>went</u> to bed.

Lesson 55: Expansion Activity

A

1. I didn't get up early yesterday.
2. It didn't rain last night.
3. They didn't make dinner.
4. We didn't go to the movies.
5. Jack didn't call me on Saturday.
6. You didn't give me a ride yesterday.

Lesson 56: Expansion Activity

A

Judy, Andy, and Mika <u>did</u> a lot last weekend. On Saturday morning, Judy <u>went</u> shopping with Mika. Andy <u>didn't go</u> shopping. He <u>was</u> at the beach. He <u>swam</u> for one hour. They all <u>met</u> for lunch at a nice restaurant. In the afternoon, Judy <u>went</u> home and studied. Andy and Mika <u>were</u> downtown. They <u>saw</u> a movie. Andy <u>didn't like</u> it. At night, Andy and Judy <u>went</u> dancing. Mika <u>stayed</u> home and <u>watched</u> TV. Everyone <u>slept</u> late on Sunday. Andy and Mika <u>made</u> a delicious breakfast. Then, Mika and Judy <u>went</u> to the park. They <u>played</u> tennis for two hours. Andy <u>didn't want</u> to play tennis. He <u>walked</u> to the supermarket and <u>bought</u> groceries. Later, he <u>cooked</u> dinner for Mika and Judy. At night, Mika, Judy, and Andy <u>were</u> at home. Mika and Judy <u>were</u> tired from tennis. They <u>went</u> to bed at 9:00. Andy <u>wasn't</u> tired. He <u>watched</u> TV until 11:00. It <u>was</u> a busy weekend!

B

Who...	Judy	Mika	Andy
...didn't go shopping on Saturday?			✓
...wasn't at the beach?	✓	✓	
...went to a movie?		✓	✓
...didn't like the movie?			✓
...wasn't downtown Saturday afternoon?	✓		
...didn't go dancing?		✓	
...slept late on Sunday?	✓	✓	✓
...didn't play tennis?			✓
...was at home Sunday night?	✓	✓	✓
...wasn't tired Sunday night?			✓

Lesson 57: Expansion Activity

A

1. Did you go to New York last year?
2. Did you take the bus to school yesterday?
3. Was it very cold?
4. Did she come to my house this morning?
5. Were you a student two years ago?
6. Were they at the beach yesterday?
7. Did I eat dinner at my friend's house last night?

8. Did we go skiing in Colorado last year?
9. Did she make a salad for the party?
10. Were there five students in the class?
11. Did we hear a lot of beautiful music at the concert?

Lesson 58: Expansion Activity

A

1. H, 2. C, 3. E, 4. I, 5. A, 6. G, 7. F, 8. D, 9. B, 10. K, 11. J

B

1. because, 2. in, 3. on, 4. by, 5. at, 6. to

Lesson 59: Expansion Activity

A

1. Did you go to the beach yesterday?
2. Was she very happy in Beijing?
3. Did he go to the beach yesterday?
4. Did they eat dinner at a restaurant last night?
5. Did Henry and Anna want to see us?

B

1. Where did you live last year?
2. How did you go to school?
3. Why was he in China?
4. Where did she study?
5. Who did Kevin marry?
6. When did they see the movie?

Lesson 60: Expansion Activity

Various answers are possible.

Lesson 61: Expansion Activity

1. I'm going to go to my friend's house tonight
2. Marion is going to stay at our house.
3. Joe and Ella are going to cook dinner for us.
4. You're going to be late for school.
5. Janet and I are going to have lunch together tomorrow.
6. Ed is going to buy a new car next year.

Lesson 62: Expansion Activity

A

Saturday and Sunday	Monday	Tuesday	Wednesday	Thursday	Friday
1/2	3	4 today	5 tomorrow	6 the day after tomorrow	7 in three days
8/9 next weekend	10 next Monday	11	12	13	14

Lesson 63: Expansion Activity

Various answers are possible.

Lesson 64: Expansion Activity

1. What time is the movie going to start?
2. Who are they going to go to New York with?
3. Why is she going to study education?
4. Where is he going to eat dinner?
5. How is she going to get here?
6. When are they going to go to Europe?
7. What am I going to eat for dinner?
8. How much is the trip going to cost?
9. How long are we going to be in Europe?
10. What am I going to do this summer?
11. What time are they going to be home?

Review Tests Answer Key

Lessons 1–4: Review Test

A

1. <u>a</u> book, 2. <u>an</u> apartment, 3. <u>a</u> table, 4. <u>a</u> mother, 5. <u>an</u> old man, 6. <u>a</u> house

B

1. we 2. it 3. they 4. I 5. you

C

1. old 2. new 3. black 4. big 5. small

D

1. On Saturdays, I <u>swim</u>.
2. I <u>live</u> in New York.
3. For fun, I <u>go</u> to a party.
4. I <u>love</u> Chicago.
5. At school, I <u>study</u> English.

E

1. New York is a big city.
2. It is an apartment.
3. He is a happy baby.
4. He is an old man.
5. I like big stores.

Lessons 5–8: Review Test

A

　　My name <u>is</u> David. I <u>am</u> from Miami. Helen <u>is</u> my wife. We <u>are</u> architects. I <u>am</u> also a student. Helen <u>is</u> the boss in her office. I <u>am</u> not the boss in my office. Helen's office <u>is</u> beautiful. Her building <u>is</u> downtown. My building <u>is</u> near my school. It <u>is</u> not downtown.

B

1. They aren't/They're not married.
2. I'm not from Chicago.
3. She isn't/She's not beautiful.
4. Mark and I aren't happy.
5. You aren't/You're not friendly.

C

1. They are friendly people.
2. She is a young teacher.
3. They aren't quiet children.
4. It is a cheap book.
5. It isn't a crowded (jewelry) store.

Permission granted to reproduce for classroom use.

D

1. David is never home on Saturdays.
2. The children are usually busy.
3. Sometimes Mike and Anna are absent from school./Mike and Anna are sometimes absent from school./Mike and Anna are absent from school sometimes.
4. Mr. and Mrs. Smith are often late.
5. Harry is always happy.

Lessons 9–11: Review Test

A

1. There are people in the class.
2. There is a big kitchen in the apartment.
3. There are a lot of kids in the neighborhood.
4. There is one teacher in my class.
5. There are children in the park.

B

1. Is the doctor a woman?
2. Is she at work or at home?
3. Is there a big tree in the yard?
4. Am I late?
5. Are there parks nearby?
6. Is he in the living room?
7. Are we on time?
8. Are there two teachers in the class?
9. Is the architect from Chicago or New York?
10. Is it cloudy?

C

1. ✓ Yes, I am.
2. ✓ No, it isn't.
3. ✓ I'm married.
4. ✓ Yes, there is.
5. ✓ No, he's not.
6. ✓ Yes, there are.
7. ✓ No, we're not.
8. ✓ She's a woman.
9. ✓ No, you're not.
10. ✓ Yes, there are.

Lessons 12–16: Review Test

A

1. This is a library.
2. Those are statues.
3. These are my books.
4. This is my closet.
5. That's a school.
6. This is a park.
7. That's a parking lot.
8. These are great pillows!
9. Those are my grandparents.
10. That's my sister.

B
1. Are these CDs?
2. Is that a stereo?
3. Are those her clothes?
4. Is this an MP3 player?
5. Are those his chairs?

C
1. Are these your books?
2. What are those?
3. What are these?
4. Is this your bedroom?
5. What's that?

Lessons 17–21: Review Test

A
1. <u>When's</u> your birthday?
2. <u>How's</u> the weather?
3. <u>Where are</u> you from?
4. <u>What time is</u> your party?/When's your party?
5. <u>How are</u> your kids?
6. <u>What's</u> your name?
7. <u>Where's</u> my wallet?
8. <u>What's</u> your first language?
9. <u>Where are</u> Anna and Paul?
10. <u>How are</u> your pancakes?

B
1. My party is <u>at</u> 7:00.
2. His birthday is <u>on</u> July 2.
3. My trip is <u>in</u> August.
4. The meeting is <u>at</u> 8:00 in the morning.
5. Her flight is <u>on</u> September 22.

C
1. ✓ It's Tom.
2. ✓ It's sunny.
3. ✓ They're on the table.
4. ✓ New York.
5. ✓ Mexican.
6. ✓ English.
7. ✓ It's on Saturday.
8. ✓ It's at 3:00.
9. ✓ It's not very good.
10. ✓ They're busy.

Lessons 22–26: Review Test

A
1. J, 2. E, 3. G, 4. H, 5. F, 6. B, 7. I, 8. D, 9. C, 10. K, 11. A

B

1. from, to
2. on
3. at
4. on
5. in

C

1. their
2. There
3. They're
4. Their
5. They're

D

1. __✓__ She's fifteen years old.
2. __✓__ She's my mother.
3. __✓__ It's two hours long.
4. __✓__ It's $8.00.
5. __✓__ It's at 3:00.

Lessons 27–30: Review Test

A

1. Helen__'s__ friend is here.
2. Harry__'s__ happy today.
3. The chair__s__ are in the kitchen.
4. It__'s__ over there.
5. His son__'s__ name is Gary.

B

1. __✓__ Helen is Martin's aunt.
2. __✓__ Mary is Mark's grandmother.
3. __✓__ Ann is John's niece.
4. __✓__ Charlie is Susan's brother.
5. __✓__ Mario is Roberto's cousin.

C

1. I __go__ to school every day.
2. On Wednesdays, Al and Erika __go__ to English class.
3. Erika __goes__ to the library on Sundays.
4. Every summer, we __go__ to the mountains.
5. He __goes__ there at 8:00.

D

1. Erika and I __go to__ work at 7:00.
2. They __go__ home at 5:00.
3. Lisa and Ann __go__ swimming every day.
4. I __go to the__ park with my friends.
5. You __go__ bike-riding in the summer.

Lessons 31–34: Review Test

A

1. takes 2. brushes 3. wakes up 4. eat 5. go

B

1. tries   2. watches   3. works   4. plays   5. fixes   6. stays   7. lives   8. misses
9. wakes up   10. studies

C

1. have   2. does   3. take   4. takes   5. has/makes

D

1. don't work   2. doesn't brush   3. doesn't do   4. don't play   5. don't watch

Lessons 35–38: Review Test

A

  1. Do I have homework?
  2. Does she go to work at 8:00?
  3. Do they want pizza for dinner?
  4. Does it snow a lot in January?
  5. Do you study hard at night
  6. Do they always go to bed at 10:00?
  7. Does she teach English in Chicago?
  8. Do you have to go to the restaurant?
  9. Does he like my school?
10. Is John a student?

B

  1. Do you go to school on Mondays?
  2. I always eat breakfast at 7:00.
  3. I need to buy some food.
  4. What do you eat for lunch?
  5. He never goes skiing in December.
  6. Do they go to the library?
  7. Does Katya live in San Francisco?
  8. He rarely plays baseball in the winter.
  9. I have to study every night.
10. Why do you take classes?

C

1. When is your birthday?
2. What does he eat for breakfast?
3. Where does she go in the summer?
4. Who do you live with?
5. What time does your class start?

Lessons 39–43: Review Test

A

1. is sitting
2. are playing
3. am writing
4. are swimming
5. are eating

B

1. They aren't working today./They're not working today.
   Are they working today?
2. She's not doing her homework./She isn't doing her homework.
   Is she doing her homework?
3. You're not studying hard./You aren't studying hard.
   Are you studying hard?
4. It's not raining in New York City./It isn't raining in New York City
   Is it raining in New York City?
5. I'm not going to the beach.
   Am I going to the beach?

C

1. What are they doing?
2. Why is he crying?
3. Who is babysitting?
4. When are you going skiing?/When am I going skiing?
5. Where are you going next week?

D

1. d
2. e
3. a
4. f
5. c
6. b

Lessons 44–47: Review Test

A

1. gets up
2. is
3. are coming
4. wear
5. is eating
6. take
7. plays
8. am listening
9. go
10. am working

B

1. He can't play the piano./He cannot play the piano.
   Can he play the piano?
2. She's not going to the beach today./She isn't going to the beach today.
   Is she going to the beach today?
3. They don't study English on Tuesdays.
   Do they study English on Tuesdays?
4. It doesn't rain a lot in the summer.
   Does it rain a lot in the summer?
5. They can't speak English./They cannot speak English.
   Can they speak English?

C

1. He goes skiing every winter.
2. I can speak English.
3. She can swim.
4. I can speak English, and I can speak Spanish./I can't speak English, but I can speak Spanish./I can speak English, but I can't speak Spanish.
5. He is wearing his uniform now.

Lessons 48–51: Review Test

A

1. He wasn't born in Mexico.
   Was he born in Mexico?
2. John and Ling weren't home last night.
   Were John and Ling home last night?
3. You weren't at the restaurant yesterday.
   Were you at the restaurant yesterday?
4. There wasn't a lot of rain in the summer.
   Was there a lot of rain in the summer?
5. It wasn't a good restaurant.
   Was it a good restaurant?

B

1. E   2. B   3. K   4. A   5. D   6. I   7. J   8. C   9. G   10. F   11. H

C

1. was   2. is   3. were   4. are   5. am

Lessons 52–56: Review Test

A

1. took
2. made
3. walked
4. studied
5. gave
6. put
7. stopped
8. ate
9. cried
10. went

B

1. I didn't cut the vegetables for the salad.
2. Alice didn't marry Joe.
3. Andy didn't hug his son this morning.
4. The teacher didn't smile at the children.
5. We didn't study for the test.

C
1. didn't
2. weren't
3. wasn't
4. didn't
5. weren't
6. didn't
7. didn't
8. wasn't
9. didn't
10. wasn't

Lessons 57-60: Review Test

A
1. Were there a lot of people at the park yesterday?
2. Did he go skiing in the mountains in December?
3. Did she sleep for a long time?
4. Was it sunny on Tuesday?
5. Did you drive to work yesterday?

B
1. Who did she go with?
2. Why did he get here late?
3. Where did they eat dinner?
4. How did she come here?
5. When did they go to New York?

C
1. D   2. A   3. F   4. E   5. B   6. C

D
1. is swimming
2. went
3. are
4. fly
5. is looking at
6. smiled
7. had
8. stops
9. cried
10. is

Lessons 61–64: Review Test

A
1. right now
2. tonight
3. tomorrow
4. the day after tomorrow
5. in three days
6. next month

B

Affirmative Statement	You're going to go to Los Angeles.
Negative Statement	You're not going to go to Los Angeles./ You aren't going to go to Los Angeles.
Yes-No Question	Are you going to go to Los Angeles?

Affirmative Statement	They're going to drive to work today.
Negative Statement	They're not going to drive to work today./ They aren't going to drive to work today.
Yes-No Question	Are they going to drive to work today?

Affirmative Statement	She is going to clean her room.
Negative Statement	She isn't going to clean her room./ She's not going to clean her room.
Yes-No Question	Is she going to clean her room?

C
1. When are they going to study English?
2. How long is it going to take?
3. Why is he going to go to England?
4. How are they going to go there?
5. Who is she going to eat dinner with?

D
1. Are you going to go to school?
2. I'm going to visit my friends.
3. He is not going to dance.
4. What time is she going to go home?
5. They are going to watch TV.